Applied Theatre in action
a journey

Applied Theatre in action
a journey

Jennifer S. Hartley

Foreword by Edward Bond

Trentham Books
Stoke-on-Trent, UK and Sterling, USA

Trentham Books Limited
Westview House   22883 Quicksilver Drive
734 London Road   Sterling
Oakhill   VA 20166-2012
Stoke on Trent   USA
Staffordshire
England ST4 5NP

First published 2012

British Library Cataloguing-in-Publication Data
A catalogue record for this book is available from the British Library

Cover image by James Jones, reproduced with his kind permission

ISBN 978-1-85856-496-8

Designed and typeset by Trentham Books Ltd, Chester
Printed and bound in Great Britain by 4edge Limited, Hockley

For Joseph Munyambanza and Benson Wereje

Contents

Acknowledgements

I gave up on writing this book more than once, questioning its value and myself as a practitioner. Had it not been for the unwavering support and guidance of David Davis this book would not exist. I thank him for his patience, hours of work and long talks, his advice, his belief in the work I do and, most of all, I thank him for his friendship.

None of the projects discussed in this book, or the many that did not make it onto these pages, could exist without the many and varied groups I have worked with over the years. I have been privileged to work around the world on inspiring projects, meeting extraordinary people who have shaped my work and influenced my life. I owe a debt of gratitude to all these people for the trust they have placed in me and the work, for their support and for all that they have taught me.

Over the years I have had the opportunity to work with so many people who have taught with me and supported me in my work. Every project has a team behind it and these people are mentioned briefly in each chapter. Without them I would never have been able to do the work I do. The teams are varied and spread out around the world.

From the UK and around Europe I would like to thank Suzanne Phillips, Jason Camilleri, Luke Jacobson, Dinos Aristidou, Michael TM Hartley, Dorte Rambo, Paddy Faulkner, Zoe Goodacre, Andrea Hodges, Simon Morgan-Thomas, Jessica Naish, Kwesi Johnson, Christopher Rees and finally, James Jones for his sensitive documentation of much of my work through his photography (including the cover work of this book).

From the US and South America I would like to thank John Spencer, Ian Madden, Bill Koehnlein, Nelson Viveros, Emilio Barreto, Virgilio Barreiro, Meli Rockhold, Sebastian Jimenez, Connor Hughes, Lynne Parish, Maria Ines Sala, Victor Bogado, Gang Initiatives, and Arts in Prisons. I also owe a debt of gratitude to Augusto Boal for his teachings and the various opportunities to work with and learn from him.

From Africa and Asia I would like to thank Benson Wereje, Joseph Munyambanza, Gavin Peter, Abdi Olawo, Zane Lucas, Kenneth Cheng, Nicolas Qing, Johanna Lindberg, DJ Donald, CIYOTA, *Ibyiringiro Bisha* (New Hope) Theatre Group, Theory X, White Fingers, Forum Syd, The African Leadership Academy.

No acknowledgements would be complete without thanking my parents for their support and for never asking too many questions about where I am going and what I am doing!

I would also like to thank Edward Bond for his support in taking the time to write the foreword to this book. Finally, I must thank Trentham publishers for their patience and support throughout this entire process. In particular I would like to thank Gillian Klein who has graciously and generously given her time to prepare this book for publication and been so supportive throughout the writing process.

Foreword
I don't accuse
Edward Bond

This book is part autobiography, part instruction manual and part history of our times.

It is the autobiography of a young woman who went into parts of the world to face dangers from beasts and people that we would flee. She freely entered the prisons of other people's lives – iron-and-cement prisons of political tyranny but also the more treacherous prisons (the oubliettes of modern democracy, in fact) of poverty, cultural deprivation and economic corruption. If she had been a cat, to survive she would have needed a hundred and nine lives.

It is an instruction manual not on how to understand the victims, and even from time to time donate to a helping charity, but on how the victims may come to understand themselves. Charity, after all, never escapes the corruption of our present market culture. Instead it is necessary to understand that the victims' own experience is more profound than that of their helpers. All that the helpers can do is to help the victims to understand their own experience, and above all to know that they have the right to understand it and to understand themselves. All tyrants, all agents of deprivation, know that to retain their power the one essential thing to do is remove that right from the victims. When the right is restored the victims will know how to speak and act for themselves. But without that right nothing can help them.

The instruction manual is the tools of drama. Without these tools there is no humanness, because self-knowledge does not come by rote, it cannot be taught, and only the self can create its own self-autonomy. It is as if incomprehension and even ignorance must create knowledge out of itself. How can that be? It can be done only when the self is free to dramatise its own experience, to confront and unwind the situations that bind it, to use the pains of repression to open the doors of freedom. That is difficult and a lot of this book is about devising and ceaselessly improving the dramatic methods needed to do it. To give the victims the mandate of drama.

The history of our times is a catalogue of prisons. They are state prisons patrolled by armed guards or market-democracies sustained by manufactured impotence and smiling salesmen. The former are serviced by torturers working in cells, the latter by family violence in homes and inter-gang violence on city streets. This book makes shockingly clear that there is no moral distinction between police-state torture and the violence fostered by market democracies. Both are caused by deprivation and repression. It is the book's most important lesson. We cannot accuse, we stand accused.

And because that is increasingly so, it is difficult to understand and remedy the situation common to East and West. It is a world prison and only the prison governors don't know this. Changing a state tyranny into a market-democracy will remedy nothing. Liberal democracy deludes itself when it thinks it will. It will only clutter the world with more weapons and confuse it with the mendacious and impoverishing prosperity of its corrupt markets.

This is the sort of book that each reader will make his or her own. Alerted by its urgency they will find in it what they need. For me these are the shocking, awesome illuminations suddenly created by drama that has been honed to be implacable, ruthless, precise and tender. These illuminations occur throughout the book. Read the account of the torturer, the spit and the handkerchief. Because of the handkerchief, the victims, Jennifer Hartley and her colleagues – and the torturer – there is hope.

Preface

The nights in Africa are the blackest I have experienced. Normally our eyes become accustomed to the dark and we can begin to see our way, but on a moonless African night this is impossible for me and my co-facilitators – the white people – as we embark on our theatre projects deep in northern Uganda, the 'Pearl of Africa', where the wild terrain borders its warring neighbour, the Democratic Republic of Congo. While the Africans manoeuvre their way around the holes in the road, the fallen trees and the ditches, we trip, fall and lose our direction. Our friends in the refugee camp chorus an apologetic 'sorry' each time, the tradition being to apologise when someone has an accident regardless of who or what caused it. They joke that this is a tradition they need to disregard, because we don't stop stumbling and falling. On the nights we work late in the camp they always accompany us back to the mission dwellings where we stay, concerned by our inability to negotiate the winding paths in the dark and because Africa, they tell us, is not a safe place to travel in at night.

Over the years of working on projects in African countries, I have heard and heeded the warning never to travel at night, but familiarity breeds a dangerous sense of security and an arrogant belief in one's own indestructibility. In August 2010, for the first time in our travels to the camp, we decided to travel from the camp to Entebbe international airport through the night – a journey that could take anything from seven to twelve hours depending on the state of the roads. My justification for this decision was the money and time it would save to avoid travelling to Kampala the day before and the costly overnight stay in the city. After three years of working in the Kyangwali Refugee Settlement, I thought I was familiar with the journey and the troubles the road can cause, especially after heavy rain. From the camp to the nearest major town, Hoima, is roughly a two-hour journey if the dirt roads are intact, followed by a four-hour drive to Kampala on properly built roads and a further hour to the airport. Travelling at night would avoid the traffic hold ups near Kampala, famous for its chaotic traffic jams, and a direct route into the airport for our early morning flight.

Travelling through the night in the city, while feasible, is ill advised, but the journey through the forests between the refugee camp and Hoima is dangerous and only undertaken when there is no other option. I only know that now.

The refugees listened to our plan and said nothing to us; their respectful way of expressing disagreement. Much heated discussion followed in one of the many languages we do not speak that are common currency in a camp that hosts approximately 25,000 refugees from various countries and tribes, meaning that roughly twenty languages are spoken in the settlement. Then we were informed – not asked – that one of the refugees would travel with us. They were distrustful of our driver, a Ugandan national who spoke little English, and felt we would be safer with Moises there, a refugee from the Democratic Republic of Congo (DRC). We agreed, comforted by the fact that we had a translator but otherwise unconcerned about the late night travelling.

It was only when the journey began that we learned Moises did not speak Lugandan, the main language used in Uganda, and his concept of translating was to speak English louder and slower than we did. When I questioned Moises on the futility of this, not to mention his uselessness as a translator, he simply shrugged his shoulders and said that he and the driver were both African and so would instinctively understand one another.

Working in Africa you get used to the seemingly nonsensical explanations, the apparent matter of fact statements that catch you off guard. It is a world of opposites, where I constantly have to check myself for misunderstanding or being offended by statements intended as compliments, and the directness and honesty that would be considered rude elsewhere. Most people seem to have a matter of fact view of their existence and the difficulties they face, an acceptance that I find both frustrating and humbling.

During this visit to the camp, for instance, the group I was working with sat in uncharacteristic silence when they saw me again. When I quizzed them about this they told me they were surprised to see how successful I had become and they must respect my superiority. I stood there bemused by this statement, dressed in filthy clothes from the long journey, dishevelled and badly in need of a shower. They then explained: 'You must be successful because you have become fat!' I was offended and tried to explain that while I may have put on weight since my last visit, I most certainly was not fat. It was their turn to look bemused; for them the heavier you are, the more successful you must be. For people who are suffering from starvation, it is a sign that you are able to eat well. They had tried to praise me and, not for the first time, I was left licking my wounds from their compliments.

After the usual lengthy goodbyes, we began our journey from the camp at around 1am. We calculated that if we left just after midnight we would arrive at Entebbe airport around 7am, and even earlier if the forest roads had not been washed away by the rain. The driver had not slept, despite our concerns that he would be too tired to make the long journey and negotiate the bad roads which demanded a high level of alertness. He was clearly unhappy with our plan and very vocal about it – however his objections remained unclear because he spoke so little English. I felt he was being difficult and unneces- sarily dramatic, a common ploy to extract more money from the *mzungos* (white people). But I considered myself an experienced traveller in Africa and would not be taken in by such things – an arrogance for which I was about to pay dearly.

The road out of Kyangwali had been improved from its state a few weeks earlier when we arrived; a journey that had taken three times longer than normal and had seriously damaged the minibus we travelled in. The UN had sent in machinery to rebuild the road until the next heavy rains but this was the only part of the road they were responsible for and the rest remained in poor condition. The road outside Kyangwali camp, linking it to Kyangwali town, was still all but destroyed from the heavy rains. We crawled along the road, scraping in and out of holes, weaving from one side of the road to the other, trying to avoid getting stuck in the ditches where the rainwater had built up. Dipping in and out of the holes with such frequency soon made us all motion sick. Our nausea was not helped by the driver cursing us every inch of the journey.

Finally we reached an improved stretch of the dirt road and picked up speed to about thirty miles an hour. After the slowness of the earlier drive we felt as if we were speeding along like rally drivers. As we made our way through the forest we suddenly saw a lone figure walking ahead of us. Moises turned to me and, in his usual cheerful and animated voice, casually informed us we would not stop and pick up this lone hiker because there were no homes in this area of the forest. This meant, he explained, that the man was probably a bandit and if we stopped the other bandits would come running out of the forest and 'chop our heads off'. Then he turned back and continued searching for an audible radio station.

Me: Chop our heads off?

Moises: Yes.

Me: Can't they just steal our stuff?

Moises: Well of course! They will do that. But they can't leave witnesses for the police, especially not a *mzungo*!

Suddenly we were all wide awake and although somewhat disconcerted, were comforted by the belief that surely Moises wouldn't be so dismissive of the danger, nor would he have agreed to accompany us, had he felt there was any real threat. We drove on, undecided whether we should be alarmed or amused by Moises's remark.

Just as I was finally starting to relax and doze off, lulled by the now familiar waving motion of the damaged road, we hit a roadblock. It was a deserted stretch of road that had been barricaded with fallen trees, crates and pieces of wood. Our problem was not knowing who the barricade belonged to. If it was a military checkpoint and we failed to stop and get out, the soldiers would shoot. But if it wasn't the military, then in all probability bandits were working the area and we were in trouble. We peered out of the windows, but it was pitch black except for a smoky haze created by the headlights. The night seemed unusually still and our nervous driver kept his foot on the accelerator, revving the engine every so often while calling out warily to see who was at the checkpoint.

We sat there for what seemed like an eternity though it couldn't even have been a minute. The driver had his window down and was leaning out trying to see if anyone was around. Suddenly a man came running from the forest screaming and waving a machete, aiming directly for the driver. With barely a second to spare, the driver instinctively pulled his arm in. He got his window up just as the man brought the machete down on the side of the car with a mighty clash of metal. We were in bandit territory and we were in trouble.

The man who had approached the car was screaming at the driver to turn off the engine and for all of us to get out, especially the white people whom he had now gleefully spotted in the back of the car. White people were a signal that there would be something worth robbing. He shouted towards the forest and suddenly from behind the trees on every side machete-wielding bandits began running towards us.

This all happened in seconds, but the thought process I went through seemed to last a lifetime. My first thoughts were, if we get out they will take everything we own: money, passports, luggage, my laptop, my camera, my ipod, my flash disc. I was thinking how I hadn't backed up the music on my ipod, that all my notes were on the laptop but backed up on the flash disc and I couldn't afford to lose both. I wondered if I could bargain with them to let me keep the flash disc. As I resigned myself to losing everything, I wondered if there was a way to at least hide my passport somewhere on my body so I could get out of the country. All these thoughts came rushing to my mind and then dissolved in reality. If we get out of this car they will rape me, the only female in the group, and then they will kill us. To leave witnesses, especially white ones, would be too great a risk. In the seconds that had passed, the car was now surrounded, with machetes being brought down hard on the car roof.

People say your life flashes before your eyes in the moments you come face to face with death. In my experience of being in such situations more frequently than most, I find that it makes you very practical, as your brain searches for a solution, a way out of the situation. You freeze at first as your brain processes what is happening and comes to a decision whether fight or flight is the best option, with flight usually winning. Your brain isn't even aware what it is doing.

We all looked at one another and knew we were thinking much the same, forming an agreement on our next move without a word being spoken. The only thing to do was to storm the barricade and hope the car would survive the impact … or that there was no truck blocking the other side of the barricade … or that we didn't get a puncture … or that they didn't set up chase. What we knew was that if we stayed we would all shortly be dead.

My heart was beating so loudly it felt as if it was outside my body. Our driver slammed his foot down on the accelerator and stormed through the barricade as fast as he could, veering slightly into the ditch at the side to minimise the impact to the car. We made it through. The car was damaged but the tyres appeared intact and we drove off at high speed. The bandits didn't even try to chase us, though that didn't stop us looking back for the next hour in fear they would suddenly reappear. We drove on in silence, taking in what had just happened, until suddenly Moises began to narrate the entire incident to us. With great excitement, he recounted all that had just occurred as if we hadn't been there, even though we featured largely in his story. Finally he mused:

> Moises: Uganda is getting more and more like the DRC with this kind of thing. Only in the DRC they would have used machine guns not machetes and we'd all be dead now. Jennifer, you should learn, this is what happens if you insist on travelling at night.

Me: Why didn't you say that before? Why didn't you tell us it was too dangerous to travel at night?

Moises: You never asked.

...

Over the last fifteen years I have been spat on and punched; I have had my life threatened at knife point, gunpoint and by machete wielding bandits; I have been scratched by a rabid bat, chased by packs of rats – on more than one occasion – and bitten by spiders; I have been cursed by witch doctors and had spells cast upon me, which I went to unbelievable lengths to have removed; I have several times been caught in civil conflict and was implicated in a conspiracy that resulted in the fatal shooting of a vice-president.

The world of applied theatre does not require any or all of the above either as a form of initiation or as part of one's working practice. My work in applied theatre has however led me to projects with unconventional settings and groups. I did not plan to do this for a living and am constantly surprised to find myself in the situations I do or perhaps by my inability to avoid them. Friends and family constantly joke that nobody ever wants to take a vacation with me lest they may find themselves in the middle of a war zone or a natural disaster. So how did I find myself working on applied theatre projects across five continents with groups ranging from torture victims in South America to refugees in Africa?

I have never considered myself a theatre person nor a political person, yet I have been labelled as both. For many people, theatre and politics define what I do, yet both labels sit uncomfortably with me. In the 1990s I fell into theatre and never quite found my way back out. Over the years I blagged my way from one job to another based on my theatre knowledge which was probably fairly minimal. As I wrote that sentence I hesitated over using the word blag so checked it in the dictionary. It is defined as the ability 'to gain ... through confidence trickery or cheekiness. Lying is also acceptable.' I like that. And am forced to stay with the word as the most accurate description of my early theatre career.

The result has been the constant belief that I was a fake in a world of experts, that I had nothing to offer that was new or different. It was only after years of blagging that I realised I wasn't actually blagging anymore. Each experience over those years had led me to develop myself within the world of theatre. I spent years establishing myself in the academic world of theatre only to discover I had no real desire to be there. My work and passion is, and always has been, the practice of applied theatre and the development of that practice through the projects with which I became involved.

By the mid 1990s I was producing and directing theatre first in the UK and then in South America, a position I fell into, yet again more by accident than planning, not to mention a lot of blagging. My main work centred on directing musicals and actor training. I ran a large theatre group, trained young actors and was frequently heard and seen on radio and television. I hasten to add that in South America that is not as impressive as it may sound. But despite my success, I felt frustrated by the world in which I moved. Something was lacking. In South America, especially in Paraguay, I was surrounded by the effects of post-dictatorial leadership and, despite its screaming presence, the silence that accompanied it. My work was so removed from the people's reality. Of course theatre can serve many purposes and the work I was doing provided an escape, pure entertainment, but it said nothing about the reality of life under dictatorial rule or its aftermath.

My discomfort was increased by the knowledge that I was working in a country where the recent dictatorship appeared to be forgotten, a consequence of the silence that had accompanied it. Few had been brought to trial for crimes against humanity and there was an uneasy existence between those who had openly supported the dictatorship and those who had been persecuted by it. In Paraguay, where I was first based, few books existed that wrote about the dictatorship overthrown just three years prior to my arrival, no theatre explored it and those who had suffered under it maintained their uneasy silence. As a newcomer to the country it would have been easy to lead an existence oblivious to the horrors of the past and blind to its results in the present and for a long time this is what I did. Yet there was always something under the surface, an uneasiness that threatened to disturb the precarious balance that prevailed.

My fascination with this led first to writing a play exploring family and social relationships in the country based on what I had observed there. This play, *Cabezas Dislocadas* (*Dislocated Heads*) offended a large cross section of the public and provoked damning praise that I must be a liar to claim I had written it, as only a Paraguayan would be able to understand and write about such things. In my youthful naivety I saw this as something to gloat about, at least until a member of the public came up to me after a performance one evening and punched me in the face for writing a play that was offensive to his country and his people. A black eye and swollen jaw afforded me some much needed time for contemplation of my future career.

After this I turned to the world of academia and embarked on a series of investigations that were embodied in a dissertation for a fellowship and which in turn led to a doctorate. I learned quickly that my desire was not so much to create theatre as to use theatre to explore the past, its effects on the present and the possible future. In order to investigate this closely I found myself coming back to notions of what was to become formalised later in my practice as applied theatre.

Working in post dictatorship South America, the names of educationalist Paulo Freire and theatre practitioner Augusto Boal frequently arose. I had worked with Boal's Theatre of the Oppressed (TO) in my earlier studies but had gleaned little more than a superficial understanding of his work. I had struggled through his books in search of a coherent structure or plan of approach. For me, Boal was little more than the man who wrote a book of games I often used in my work. And then I was fortunate enough to meet him and came into first hand contact with his training and his work in action.

Working with TO my understanding grew of the socio-political role of theatre and how it could speak for, rather than at, communities. I began to see how theatre could become a conversation, an art that included the spectators and did not separate those on stage from those observing. TO was just the beginning. I started to combine it with my training in other aspects of theatre and with being a counsellor. I gained greater understanding of Boal and his work and this helped me discover my own direction in theatre or, perhaps more accurately, what my direction clearly was not, and this brought me into the applied theatre arena. I learned more about applying theatre methods to real people in real situations for purposes of exploration, understanding and empowerment. My interest in the socio-political aspect of theatre began to grow.

Training with Boal and seeing his work in action gave me deeper understanding of TO and its purposes. Working in post dictatorial South America provided a setting in which to develop a greater understanding of the origins of TO and what Boal was trying to do. Boal was a presence, a showman who worked his students and audiences with the suavity of a circus ringmaster. Watching the methods in action brought clarity to what I had read in his books and brought my previous studies into focus. It also led me to question many aspects of his work. There were concerns that many of the methods could be viewed as playing with people, their issues and emotions. I questioned the ultimate goal of many of the exercises and what after-care took place.

Over time I was able to take what I had learned and develop it into methods that became my own practice in applied theatre. I found myself combining the strongest elements of the practices I had been exposed to over my years of studying and working in theatre. The ability to extract from different relevant practices is something which defines the evolving practice of applied theatre for most practitioners. However I cannot deny that the foundation for my work has been Boal's TO and while I have developed this in a way that may not resemble his initial intentions, or in a way that purists of the form would still consider TO, it has helped build the foundations for my own experimentation and practice.

I recognised that applied theatre required a mix of practices and a development of those selected. It could never stand still. TO, while well established, was often restrictive in its form despite claiming to promote empowerment, freedom and participation. And I felt that TO needed to continue evolving in many different directions if it was to speak to the times in which it was now being used.

I became engaged with various projects and initiated others throughout this period, each time developing my approaches to applied theatre. My work involved dealing with ideas of perception and trying to avoid judgement about people and situations, focusing on a dialogue as opposed to searching out solutions to the problems and issues I came across. While I still directed and wrote for theatre I did so based on the work I was doing in my applied theatre projects, developing a participatory theatre spoken by the people involved, and not simply for them.

The outcome was that I started an applied theatre group just over a decade ago which came to be known as Theatre versus Oppression (TVO). Our goal was to use applied theatre with people in places where oppressive issues had been identified and where the people were looking for a new approach to dealing with them. Our work brought us into contact with the most varied groups in countries around the globe. Some were involved in theatre, but many were not. I declared that I would never go looking for a project but would see what crossed our path, as I was well aware of the suspicion that people bring to new approaches and ideas, especially when they involve the arts. Over the years the work grew, until in 2007 we became a UK registered charity dedicated to the use of applied theatre.

We have worked in schools, colleges and universities, prisons, hospitals, refugee camps, community support venues and theatres. Those who have trained or worked with us include theatre practitioners, actors, directors, designers and writers, social workers, police, educators, aid workers, therapists, youth workers, rehabilitation officers, counsellors, as well as groups united by their own experience of, or involvement in, a specific issue.

TVO also engages in performance pieces, most often the production of plays based on the project work in which we have been involved. The goal of the plays is usually to launch or promote discussion and debate, to present differing perspectives and gain broader understanding of the issue involved. Depending on how the projects grow, productions are performed by the people who have been engaged in its development. Performing their stories on stage often generates catharsis, a sense of liberation. Other plays are performed by professional casts and presented to the general public in the guise of issue-based plays for the community. Performance in applied theatre work is an active participatory role for all involved, from the actors on stage to the audience watching. It is the nature of that involvement that transforms it into applied theatre and all it brings.

I have worked with a number of people over the years and many are mentioned in the chapters that follow. Some are volunteers with TVO, some are people I have come across in the field and built a working relationship with, and some are resident workers with the groups undertaking a project. There are people I have worked with for a single project, or on projects based in a certain location or a certain issue, and there are people who have worked with me across numerous projects. In the book, the members of the team are often referred to peripherally but the contribution of the team and the need for their presence is never forgotten and always central.

I hope this book will make my journey through the world of applied theatre accessible – not only to those working in theatre, but also to the world beyond that of theatre practitioners, for the key to applied theatre lies in its inclusivity. Given the hybrid and interdisciplinary nature of applied theatre, any book on the subject should also be readily understood and embraced by other practitioners who might consider how this practice can be integrated into their own work.

Introduction

This book describes a journey through a selection of projects undertaken around the world, the background to them, the approach and
methods used, the problems encountered and the outcomes. Sometimes these experiences have produced a rapid learning curve, as in the
incident with which I began this book. I have tried to give the flavour of these
sometimes difficult, sometimes precarious, experiences, not out of bravado
but as a riposte to some writers on applied theatre who have merely observed
the work, not lived it. And I have tried to extrapolate for readers what made
the projects work.

The projects have in common the use of applied theatre to aid a process of
transformation. They aim to help people who are unable or afraid to express
themselves to discover their voice. I have chosen not to take a theoretical
approach (see Nicholson, 2005) not to present an overview of different approaches to applied theatre (see Prendergast and Saxton, 2009). These approaches have their uses but I want to give a view from the ground: to tell you
about a journey. That is why I have chosen a narrative style and inserted
stories that illustrate aspects of the reality of working in the field.

Each chapter introduces a project, recounts aspects of the work and relates
the actions and reactions of the people involved. Every project is a book in
itself, so I can only describe a few of the exercises used in it. I have changed
some names, or used only the first names of those I worked with or came into
contact with through the projects, to protect their privacy.

Chapter One explores a project designed to work with torture victims and ex
political prisoners in South America who had been silenced by the dictatorial
rule under which they had suffered. Years later, although now under democratic rule, these people found themselves still unable to discuss their experiences, after being silenced for so long first by the regime and then by their
own self-repression and fear. This project led to a briefer project with those

who had been involved in the regime mainly as prison guards and torturers. The goal at each stage of the project was to uncover the story of the individual and the behaviour they had exhibited. The people's silence and lack of understanding had left many with a fear that it could easily happen again, a terror grounded in the knowledge of how events had unfolded in their own lives. Only through open discussion and recording of their stories did they feel their past could be respected and serve a greater purpose. Applied theatre became the vehicle through which this could occur.

In Chapter Two we travel across the Atlantic to look at a project aimed at bringing harmony among rival gangs and encouraging forms of expression that did not include fatally wounding their antagonist. This project faced numerous challenges, not least the participants' frequent requests in the initial stages to be given a jail sentence rather than attend the workshops! Working in the USA presented a greater language barrier, as participants struggled with my Scottish accent, than working with African translators in Uganda in a room where eight different mother tongues were spoken.

Chapter Three moves closer to home to look at a project working with disenfranchised and 'problem' youth in the UK. Working with youth often presented more challenges and difficulties than working in the remotest of locations at the other end of the world and has often been more threatening. It necessitates the building of trust in a distinct manner from other groups, in order to help young people find a way to express themselves at a time when they are trying to discover their own voices. Too often we forget the challenges facing us on our own doorstep. These projects are a powerful reminder that the difficulties facing a first world country have more in common with third world communities than one might think.

Chapter Four examines a recent and ongoing domestic abuse project that seeks to give voice to both victim and perpetrator and help people understand their own actions and reactions. This project includes work in prisons as well as with support groups. It has produced unexpected and surprising results and it shows how prevalent domestic abuse is around the world whatever the culture, language or beliefs.

Chapter Five looks at the development of our work in Africa which has spawned a range of projects in different countries. Applied theatre has taken me to Mugabe's Zimbabwe where we were forbidden to use the words 'oppression' or 'oppressed' on the grounds that apparently nobody in Zimbabwe suffered any form of oppression; to a remote training project in Tanzania initially stalled by the participants' lack of sobriety; to a peace campaign for the youth in Kenya's Rift Valley; and finally to one of our longest standing and ongoing projects with the Kyangwali Refugee Settlement in northern Uganda. Africa has presented us with new challenges in our work, both personally and as practitioners. The difficult living conditions, sickness and instability in each location has necessitated a new approach to our work and the way we set up projects, as well as forcing us to live and work in conditions well beyond our normal comfort zones.

Throughout this book I allocate the terms he/she randomly.

Games and exercises

Games feature largely in my work. 'Game' is a disarmingly simple term. We use the word in so many contexts that it is familiar and recognisable. Through my work I have come to discover how complex games can be. The distinguishing line between games and exercises can be difficult to draw, creating a grey area around what one might call an activity, a game or an exercise. How we approach a game can quickly turn it into an exercise, adding new layers. The principal difference between them is that exercises are formulated to infuse a given structure with genuine content. For me exercises are the building blocks of a project. Through them I explore the topic or issue of the project with the participants and allow them to interrogate possibilities of how they feel and where they want to go with the work. Exercises invite exploration and experimentation. They are designed to enable people to work with a particular theme and to discover more about it and about themselves in relation to it. One exercise will build upon another, based on the response of the group to each exercise and how they develop it. So no two projects are ever the same.

Games on the other hand serve to build relationships while de-mechanising the body. They help free us from habitual behaviour, as a prelude to moving beyond habitual thinking and interacting. From the perspective of the facilitating team, games also serve as checkpoints to observe and learn about the group, and to provide a break from the exercises, which can be extremely demanding physically, emotionally and mentally.

Games play a significant role in all my work. In theatre, games are too often used randomly, chosen for the fun of it, or as a time filler. In my own approach to applied theatre there is nothing random in either the timing or the selection of the games to be played. During my first meeting with a group I play games with no apparent relation to any issue or possible problem area the project will be focusing on. In that first session I am reading the group, the dynamics, personal relationships and issues within it, as well as underlying issues and areas of concern. Games are specifically tailored to each group, otherwise it could prove extremely difficult to engage the participants. The key is to help participants reach a point where they are no longer self-aware within the games, no longer worrying what they look like or what other people are thinking about them. Not surprisingly, this is often more difficult with young people, who tend to be highly image conscious, than with adults.

Games are selected that will build up the ensemble aspect of the group. Each participant begins working with a partner. Normally they immediately select someone they know and feel comfortable with. But they are asked to change partners with each exercise, and are not allowed to work with the same person twice. This helps the facilitator to see at once who is being avoided or excluded by the others, the people the group are reticent to work with for one reason or another. The reasons reveal themselves as the games continue. The opening games also establish who the cliques are, as they will work hard to change partners only within their own group, until they have exhausted all possible options.

From here the games will alternate between small group and whole group work. I take care with the introduction of whole group work as many games in this area can result in one person being singled out, for example in the centre of a circle. A mixture of self-consciousness and image-consciousness can make for very reluctant participants. Young people can resent being made to feel they are in the spotlight, especially if they are unsure about what is being asked of them, or are not particularly adept at the activity. I tend to avoid any whole group exercises at the start, unless they require everyone in the group to be doing things at the same time, meaning that the spotlight is not on any one person.

Through the games certain personality types will emerge and recognising this helps guide me in how future exercises and games are selected. Natural leaders emerge quickly, and differ from attention seekers who can initially come across as potential leaders. The quiet, shy ones also emerge, who struggle to find their voice within the group. There can be various reasons why people are quiet, ranging from simple shyness to serious causes such as abuse. Games allow for non-intrusive investigation. Both bullying and victim personalities surface in game work. Resistance to the issue behind the purpose of the workshop will occasionally surface at this stage, even though the issue is not yet being dealt with. This early defensiveness, even aggressiveness, can be a sign of a personal issue or fear and should not be ignored. Gauging reactions can be integrated into game activities to allow for non-intrusive and more extensive investigation.

During my first meeting with the group but after they have played for some time, I introduce games that require them to begin expressing their thoughts and opinions. Having watched the group and how they interact, I am now aiming to get a reading on what they feel about certain things, what subjects they are passionate about, what matters are troubling them. It also helps me see how they express themselves and their ideas. Games allow for participants safely to make commentaries to us about their situation, the workshops, and even how they feel towards us as facilitators.

With adults I often use games to stop them over-processing an exercise. With young people the games can become an incentive to get through challenging work. As the facilitator, it is my job to play what will appear like random games, but which are actually designed to work with an issue that has arisen in the workshop and is usually related to the exercise that they have been doing. The seeming randomness and simplicity is key to the group's engagement. In reality it takes extensive planning and familiarity with a large bank of appropriate games that can be applied in the moment.

For example, in recent work with female victims of abuse, the fear of touch arose in an exercise. The more this developed, the more the women revealed about their discomfort and unwillingness, or even inability, to have physical contact with others. The topic was distressing to many so I suggested we take a break and played a game, an idea that was warmly welcomed by the participants. The game I played, called Paper Chase (all games and exercises referred to can be found in the glossary at the end of the book) involved various challenges with different partners, where there was only a sheet of paper between them. The tasks were difficult and required focus and coordination and the women forgot the close proximity they had to one another. The game is built up until finally the whole group are joined together by no more than a sheet of paper between them and the person they are working with.

The participants were so caught up in the game that they didn't realise how much physical contact was taking place. They would begin with no contact except the sheet of paper but, as the game proceeded, they would hold on to each other, to ensure they didn't lose the paper. The result was far more intimate physical contact than normal. The women laughed and joked with one another throughout and only when the game had ended did they realise what had happened. For some of them this was a breakthrough experience.

They discussed the idea that touch could be a positive experience for them once again.

When I began working with a women's safety unit, the women were extremely nervous about the workshop. In part this was because I was a stranger coming into their world, but it was also strongly related to a fear of failure. Many of the women were afraid they would be unable to do the things I asked of them. Faced with incessant criticism in their relationships, these women had extremely low self-esteem. They were quick to see themselves at fault, and highly critical of themselves as being stupid or incapable of following instructions. The games helped remove any such pressure. They also helped the women see that it was not about getting things right and that making mistakes, or struggling with some of the exercises, could be fun. Afterwards they talked about how much they had laughed and how empowering it had felt to find themselves laughing so freely.

Augusto Boal

Undeniably my work has been heavily influenced by Augusto Boal's Theatre of the Oppressed (TO), a result of the years I spent in South America and my experiences of working directly with Boal. (I have also been influenced by other theatre practices and practitioners I have studied from Brecht to Brook, Meisner to Spolin, Artaud to Stanislavski, but an elaboration of these areas would not be relevant here.) And I have always looked at my theatre work through the eyes of my training and work in counselling.

Although TO's influence has been strong, I have always approached it as a progression and exploration rather than a unified theory that can be applied unwaveringly. I do not believe that Boal's work was intended to be rigidly followed step by step without change, or that there is a single correct way of approaching it, rather that it invites experimentation and constant adaption to the particular issue, group and location. I see Theatre of the Oppressed as a way to explore ideas and progress distinctively each time the work is applied.

Boal was a performer, a one-man show and I found this entertaining and fascinating to watch but it often left me confused. So much attention was given to the man rather than the work, not only by the critics but also by the groups he worked with. The personality became larger than the practice. Other aspects of TO troubled me as well, leaving me with questions that I have since sought answers to in my own working practice.

Often in a workshop I saw more feelings aroused than could be accommodated and dealt with and I worried about what might happen to these people after they returned home. I wondered where the safety net was for those left feeling vulnerable and exposed, especially by the introspective techniques most frequently found in *Rainbow of Desire* (Boal, 1995). Boal himself frequently referred to his workshops as laboratories, which carries implications of experimenting *on* people, as opposed to exploring *with* them.

Boal talked frequently of oppression always being brought back to an individual and he was clearly more comfortable with socio-political issues where an oppressor was evident and tangible. The work always depends on an acknowledgement of the other, on the continuous exchanges with agents of social struggle. This can be seen most clearly in his early work in South America which he discusses in his book *Hamlet and the Baker's Son: my life in theatre and politics* (Boal, 2001). But it was never clear what to do when possibilities of tracing the oppressor back to an individual seemed impossible or even contradictory, as the source of the oppression would often lie both with the general concept of society and within ourselves or another person. For example, in a society obsessed with body image the expectation to look a certain way comes from society in general but also from our own expectations of ourselves and what we should look like. Those expectations have, however, been shaped by society, by the glossy magazines and airbrushed photos of models and film stars. We know they are false images yet we strive to resemble them. We would have a difficult time narrowing it down to a single person and dealing with it, selecting a single oppressor to challenge our self-dissatisfaction

I also struggled with talking about oppressors in, for instance, a refugee camp and questioned whether certain groups needed to work with this label. These are things I have challenged myself on in my own practice. Above all, I found it hard to shake off the idea that we were coming at things from a negative perspective. This is a practice aimed at empowering individuals, yet it frequently appeared to come at this through negative concepts and feelings. Even the name theatre 'of' the oppressed seems to imply a negative, a strange title for a practice that claims to empower. In our own charity organisation, Theatre versus Oppression, the use of the word 'versus' signalled our intent and beliefs (more information about Theatre versus Oppression – TVO – can be found at the end of this book).

What has most appealed to me about TO has always been how participatory it is. People who thought they could or would never act no longer felt threatened in a TO setting. I myself, who have always hated acting, feel a freedom in many of the TO exercises that enabled an acting skill to emerge that I didn't believe I had. Boal's methods present problem-solving strategies, often presenting new ways to look at old problems. They enable action, reflection and possible ways forward. It was through this praxis Boal saw possibilities to envision, rehearse and enact change for our world. Handled well, the methods raise questions and interrogate possibilities without imposing solutions. And that is the caveat: if used well, TO celebrates the playful nature in all of us that is an essential part of our humanity, but if handed poorly or in a misguided way, it can be damaging, as it uncovers issues the facilitators are ill equipped to deal with.

My approach to applied theatre

Boal's work encourages sympathy with an issue, not empathy. The idea is that sympathy enables a connection, an affiliation, without becoming lost in the issue, acknowledging feelings that are similar, rather than searching for sameness. Whereas in my work I have always striven for empathy and find concepts of sympathy condescending and unproductive. We facilitators are trying to empathise with the situation the people we work with find themselves in, not sympathise with them. In my work I place considerable emphasis on perception, and I believe empathy is an enabler to achieve it. Through empathy we place ourselves in another person's shoes to see how they view the world; sympathy implies feeling pity for someone.

By empathising we can move towards a better understanding of the issue and understand what we might do in a similar situation, in this way achieving better communication. In every aspect of my work I try to encourage a non-judgmental approach. In each project there is an intent to acknowledge where participants are in their own personal journey, without judgement on where that journey has brought them. The workshops and projects are an attempt to gain a better understanding of their journey up to that point, what has influenced and shaped it and the person each has become as a result. There is then an invitation to explore it further in a way that could bring about change, but only if and when each individual is ready to do so.

Theatre of the Oppressed seems to imply that we should want to change our oppressed situation, that we should constantly be fighting against that oppression. Whereas what matters is that people understand their situation, their behaviour and the choices they have made within that. That understanding may lead to a desire to change but it does not necessitate it. In the same way, I have struggled with Boal's idea that we can break oppression in an exercise like forum theatre. The breaking of any oppression is highly subjective and what works for one person may not work for another. I have seen many people try to break an oppression in a forum situation left feeling they have failed, only to watch someone else apparently succeed. For me forum is about exploring options. The oppression may be broken numerous times or never, but each intervention is an exploration of possibilities that can be adapted and applied by individuals as they choose.

With each group, I make it clear from the outset that we are not seeking to solve problems or find answers to questions: there are no simple answers to the complex questions often raised. Basically a project is about studying the situation the participants are in and letting them decide if they want to change it. I strongly believe there can be no judgement or preaching – however challenging this may be at times. Whether it is a room full of convicts in a prison, a room of drug addicts and alcoholics or of victims of abuse, they must feel accepted for who they are and where they are on their own journey and everyone must have the freedom to travel their own path at their own speed.

I realised very quickly that I was a practitioner not a theorist. With applied theatre the shaping of the work always seems to depend upon the participants and their collaborative role so my approach has developed accordingly. With each project I have no prior knowledge of the right means by which to realise the end. The experience of working with other groups and what I have learned from them is all I can bring to the initial shaping and development of each project. As each group works through what they want to achieve, we alter the way we might do so. In each workshop aims change and there is continual interplay between ends and means. In the same way there is continual interplay between thought and action and an intuitive process to help direct me through that. It is a cyclical process of experiential learning, and reflection is key to understanding what has occurred and how it can instruct future work.

Applied theatre is fundamentally about teamwork. The team provides support, helping sustain a project with all the demands, twists and turns it will bring. In TVO the teams are created principally according to who would be best suited to work on that particular project in light of their experience and expertise, although as a voluntary organisation, availability is always a factor. What makes the team work is the way in which the members' different strengths complement one another's.

For example when I work with 'at risk' youth, I try to ensure that the team has people who specialise in this area and are familiar with the likely obstacles we might face. I may know how to put the exercises together and create the plan but without the input of people who specialise in working with the particular group, I could easily make mistakes and misjudge what is appropriate and appealing. When we do gang work the team always has outreach workers and social workers who understand gang related problems, gang dynamics and gang speak. Everyone in the team has some form of theatre training and we have regular training sessions throughout the year that volunteers attend. The team creates a strong working relationship with those running the groups or the agents commissioning the project, and many of our volunteer staff have been drawn from this source. Their understanding and cooperation is often key to a project's success; without it, obstacles can constantly be put in the way of any development.

Before a project begins I sit down with the team and work out a plan for our first meeting with the group, and a rough plan of what we want to achieve overall. In the weeks before the project starts we research the group and the specific issue. Research can involve interviews, community visits, statistical research and so on. The information gathered informs how the project can best be planned, although changes are inevitable as the group plays a participatory role in deciding how things develop. Thorough research enables us to plan a project that has the potential to truly speak to the participants and allow them to feel a sense of ownership from the start. Failure to understand the community in which we will be working, or making assumptions about it can put a project at risk. Careful preparation is needed to provide a safe working environment for participants and facilitators.

When the project begins, we have the opportunity to get to know the group and their expectations for the project by indirectly asking certain questions through selected activities. The exercises and practices are selected according to what we believe will best benefit the participants. These exercises come from various theatre practices, as well as being influenced by counselling practices, depending on the nature of the project. In the process new activities may often be developed and existing activities may need to be adapted from their original form. Or the participants may take the work in a direction that creates new exercises unique to the group. This constant adaptation and development is one of the most exciting aspects of applied theatre. As I work with a group I am constantly seeing how an exercise can be adapted or when I need to create a new one in the moment which would work better for the immediate needs of the group. The strength of the team I work with rests in their ability to adapt effortlessly to these changes as they occur and to trust one another to accept and go with the changes.

Throughout the project the team meets after every workshop to discuss what happened that day and I explain my thinking behind any changes I made on the spot, so the other facilitators can see why I thought they were necessary and how they might be applied to future work. The team have the chance to challenge my decisions, and we plan the next session. Although we have an overall plan, it is participatory and it is the group who lead it so we must revise and plan the next session based on what has happened in the last. Consequently the final journey of the project can be quite different from what we originally anticipated. What is essential is that the theory has come out of the practice, developed and refined with every project we take on. That is what this kind of applied theatre is about.

Another purpose of these reflection and planning meetings is to share concerns, doubts, problems and even to sound off about certain things without fear that we are being judged for doing so. There are days when I feel everything I did had no effect, or found the group uncooperative or aggressive. There are days when I end a workshop feeling literally and emotionally bruised. There have been days when I cursed the group I was working with, or had more than enough of the threats or sexual innuendos that often come with gang and prison work. And there have been days where I have sworn I will never run another applied theatre project. We all have those days, but they pass quickly because of the support network and because that framework enables us to express things freely without feeling we are failures or being judged for having these moments. Reflection meetings help us to see what has happened from a fresh perspective and to support one another through these moments.

As the project develops our main aim is to know the people we are working with and to build their trust and comfort in working with the methods and the facilitators. I rarely start with lengthy introductions or questions to the people I am working with. Rather, we start by playing games, after which I talk to the group about the project and the issues we hope to look at. It is made clear from the start that they have ownership of the project and if they are unhappy with the topics or the direction in which we are heading, they participate in changing it. The agenda is flexible and will adapt to their needs and desires. Often we need to allow a sounding-off time, when the group can voice their opinions about the project, the commissioning agent who set it up, their situation and anything else they are unhappy about. I never put a time limit on this, but let it run its course. They stop talking when they have exhausted everything they wanted to say.

This book describes the kind of work applied theatre might encompass and my approach to this work. The experiences and ideas in it might inform the work of some readers but this is not a 'how to' manual for applied theatre practitioners. It is an invitation to join me on a journey through which I seek to share my personal experiences of my travels through the world of applied theatre. I hope it will engage your interest and curiosity in this area and dispel the mystery that surrounds applied theatre, who it is for and why it is used. It is my goal to explain the projects and process used through my stories, sharing my own transformative journey, giving voice to those I have had the honour and privilege of working with over the years.

1

Tortured and torturer:
a meeting of minds

March 23rd 1999 is a day most Paraguayans will remember. It was the day vice-president Luis Argaña was assassinated. Assailants ambushed his car not far from his home, peppering it with multiple rounds of gunfire before escaping. The assassination was the catalyst for *Marzo Paraguayo*, a week of bloody demonstrations and riots that ended with the president fleeing the country to seek asylum in Brazil and Paraguay forming its first ever coalition government.

The secretary of the school where I was that morning came running into the office in tears, shouting at us all to turn the radio on. The room was filled with an audible silence as we learned of the attack. It was clear that Argaña could not possibly have survived such an assassination attempt and that the dubious democracy that had existed since 1989 was now under threat. The motive behind the attack was unclear and the identity of the attackers a mystery. Within minutes, Paraguay's borders were sealed and strict controls on movement within the country were implemented.

More information began to filter through as we listened. We heard that the vice-president had been on the way to his office in the capital, Asunción. He had been fatally wounded in a grenade and shooting attack on his car. A vehicle had blocked the road so gunmen wearing camouflage uniforms, could attack. A sniper had been positioned on the balcony of an apartment overlooking the spot, to ensure that neither Argaña nor his bodyguards could escape.

It was only then that they named the street where this had occurred, a street chosen for its unusual 'V' shape that prevented escape and allowed easy access for the sniper. In that moment my heart sank as I realised this assassination was going to affect me more than anyone could ever have foreseen. The street and the balcony where the sniper had positioned himself was mine.

It took three long days for the authorities to believe I was not a part of the assassination plot. Three long days during which I had an intensive introduction to the Paraguayan penal system, or lack of it. Three days of disbelief accompanied by an uneasy awareness that people disappear terrifyingly easily in South America and the authorities are the last people one turns to for help. During those three days I learned why I should always have the number of a good lawyer on speed dial. And yet I still consider myself fortunate; my neighbour, who witnessed the assassination, has never been seen again since that fateful day.

Background

Young, arrogant and naïve best sum me up at the start of my career in applied theatre. Now, over a decade later I look back on that young woman with compassion, aware of the journey she was about to embark on, with all its lessons and learning curves, all its knocks and bruises. My journey began in South America, initially in Paraguay, commonly referred to by its more affluent neighbours as the armpit of South America.

After almost thirty-five years of political oppression and restrictions on freedom of expression under the Stroessner dictatorship (1954-1989), Paraguay entered into a democracy in February 1989. Most dictatorships work on a selective form of repression, pursuing those who openly challenge the regime or present a threat to it in any way. Stroessner's tactics in Paraguay had been different, more terrifying and far more effective as he imposed a systematic form of repression. He did not wait to be attacked or threatened; rather he randomly repressed innocent people. This instilled a fear that suffocated the desire to threaten or question the regime; a fear that lived on long after the dictatorship had been overthrown.

One of the most common expressions used by Paraguayans when asked why they did not rebel is *para qué?* (What for?) – there was no point in a country so intimidated by fear that it was viewed as a way of life, instead of an infringement of their civil liberties. The constant threat of oppression acted as a deterrent: obedience manifested in the absence of overt resistance. Moreover, with all public meetings prevented and the constant threat that anyone could be a government spy, Stroessner turned the Paraguayans into their own enemy. Fear and distrust became so prevalent that people became the unwitting allies of the dictator. Oppression was so complete that people could not only be punished but also constantly monitored to prevent them from gathering, criticising, debating or forming groups. Thought processes and the ability to question were inhibited from such an early stage that, for many, they seem to have been eliminated from their being. Even today many people are afraid to report those who went missing during the dictatorship, the countless *desconocidos* (unknown people) who disappeared from the system. By 1987 it was estimated that more than one-tenth of the population had been sent to prison in the first thirty years of Stroessner's regime.

It was natural to assume that the new democratic era would generate a desire to maintain and constructively reflect upon communal memory. Yet this did not happen. In the aftermath of the severe repression the arts and theatre were not being used as a vehicle for social recovery, to reflect upon Stroessner's regime and create a solid and comprehensible future. Working in South America at the time, what disturbed me most was the idea of the untold stories of the many who had fought against the dictatorship and been silenced by it. Now in a free climate these people remained silent, frustrated and angry at a system that failed to recognise their value.

I was working on various theatre and research projects in South America during the late 90s. Coming from a Spanish background (my maternal grandparents are from Spain) and speaking fluent Spanish had enabled me to work effectively in my chosen fields. In Paraguay I came across many who had been imprisoned or tortured under the regime. Their anger and frustration did not, as might be expected, centre on those who remained unpunished for their crimes against humanity, but rather on their not having been listened to. I began a project working with their stories, seeking not only to give them expression but to help people to speak again in a culture that had silenced them.

I had met and worked with Augusto Boal during this period. Although I had not yet formed Theatre versus Oppression (TVO), I was working with some like-minded people on small theatre projects in Paraguay, Argentina and Brazil. Mostly I was supporting other people's work, learning with and from them. The team was made up of practitioners with considerable experience of Theatre of the Oppressed, psychodrama and dramatherapy, who came together to support one another in projects. The majority of these projects centred on the problems of street children and the abusive situations surrounding them. Together we had used applied theatre techniques, principally variations and adaptations of Theatre of the Oppressed exercises to work with these groups. Assisting with these projects rather than leading them, I was able to learn what worked and try to understand why. I quickly learned the need to be flexible and let the participants lead the project, guided and supported by the facilitators. I also realised how difficult this could be, requiring an action plan that could be written and rewritten according to the outcome of each stage of the work. Participant led work was exciting and terrifying, heavily dependent on a disciplined yet intuitive approach. I was beginning to learn about disciplined intuition. The need for a strong team became apparent; a team that could adapt to changes quickly, supporting one another without egos taking over.

At this time I developed and led my first major applied theatre project based on working with torture victims. It began almost accidentally so its rapid growth caught me by surprise, as did the way that it so quickly came to define me. Influenced by Boal's work, I had been conducting research and workshops for a fellowship with Trinity College in London. The focus was the effects of dictatorial oppression on creativity in theatre, studies that were later to develop into doctoral research and my return to the UK. At the same time, separately, I was a volunteer counsellor. Through these two activities I had come into contact with many torture survivors, some of whom came from theatre backgrounds. They were fascinated by Boal's work, news of which had reached Paraguay during Stroessner's reign, but in a piecemeal fashion. Knowing I had worked with Boal, they asked if I would use some of the methods with them as a tool to explore their past and present trauma in dealing with the torture and imprisonment that had affected their lives. I agreed and began working with a group of five. I had no real awareness of what I had started, or how I was unintentionally changing my own life.

For over three years I worked on this project across four countries – Paraguay, Argentina, Chile and Brazil. In each country random groups were put together by others as word spread about what we were doing. It was an unlikely partnership: I, a westerner, still largely ignorant of the atrocities of South America's dictatorial regimes in the latter half of the twentieth century, and they, victims of those atrocities, distrusting, fearful of a regime long passed and sceptical about how theatre could serve them in any way. Yet the relationship grew and the projects developed. The goal – to give a voice to those who had been silenced by the dictatorial regime and ignored by its successors.

I remember being in New York on a theatre related project a few years later, when an elderly Cuban man approached me. After asking my name, he smiled in recognition saying, 'Yes yes, I know who you are! The torture lady! The one who listens to our stories of how they tortured us and helps free us.' I stood there, thousands of miles from the project I had begun, facing a man I had never met before. Overwhelmed by his statement, I suddenly felt weighed down by a desperate sense of helplessness and a fear of what I had begun. More than a decade later this reputation still seems to follow me wherever I go, and the weight of the burden has never lightened.

While I was pleased at the success the project enjoyed, I was also aware that I was learning and every decision I made affected many others, especially any mistake I made. Only later did I come to appreciate that in applied theatre this never changes. Every project is different and that is the only certainty you begin and end with. Years later it is this project in South America that continues to define my work for many. No matter how much I try, this is something I am unable to break free from. It is the most difficult project for me to speak about, partly because of all it entailed and partly because of the mistakes I feel I made. I try to remember what I always tell the students I train, 'Working in this kind of theatre means you must never forget to be kind to yourself'.

In this first major project, I established approaches that have since come to define my work in applied theatre. The first was to tie in a performance to the project, created from working with the people involved in the issue. This concept has been adapted and has taken many forms over the years and is discussed in later chapters. In this project it took the form of two plays that were created. These plays were then used to further develop the project in new ways in other communities, as discussed later in this chapter.

The second significant approach is the emphasis I place on the concept of perception and the role it plays in our stories and how we interpret them. I frequently seek to work with those involved in all sides of an issue – the parent and the child, the victim and the perpetrator, the gang member and the police – although that is not always possible or feasible. For that reason working with those who had been imprisoned and/or tortured under South American regimes only told one part of the story. I also worked with those who had tortured them. It was not about judging right or wrong, but rather about encouraging an understanding of ourselves and others, as well as an acknowledgement of different perceptions, if not acceptance of them.

Life is not simple, with clear demarcations between good and bad, black and white. In reality issues are rarely clear-cut. People often insist that I must take a stance on right and wrong in my work. They say I must make judgements about what is best or right for people and promote it. But that is not what the work is about. I do not tell people how to behave; I explore their behaviour with them. I do not tell them something is right or wrong; I explore perceptions of right and wrong within a given context. It is a journey we take together. The projects are about exploration and discussion and to be able to do that effectively it is necessary to let things develop as directed by the participants, not enforce a code of behaviour or a particular perception from the outset. But this, as will become evident, is often easier said than done.

Working with torture victims: restoring dignity

As I began this project with torture survivors, I was constantly struck by their frustration and anger at having been silenced by an oppressive regime, and by their continued, now self-inflicted, silence. Theoretically, the current democracy should have offered release for them to tell their stories.

Realising how difficult it was for many to talk openly of their experiences, I formed a small group of volunteers who had been torture victims, at their request. The group was completely male, not because women were not tortured by the regime, though statistically the numbers were comparatively low, but because these were people I already had access to. We met once a week in what had been the school hall of a now abandoned building. The aim was to use my experience as a counsellor combined with applied theatre techniques to explore their past and present. It was the beginnings of an attempt to understand the silence which had engulfed a nation. The concept was bigger than I had imagined or properly understood. As word spread, the group grew.

We met over several months and explored aspects of their situation, using a variety of Theatre of the Oppressed and counselling methods. Some members of the group came out of curiosity, others seized it as an opportunity to be heard. All were suspicious. The more I worked with them, the clearer it became that their current silence was related to a sense of fear. Fear that the dictatorship not only might return, but that it still existed under the surface. Silence was feeding that fear, so the applied theatre approach was designed to look at ways of breaking that silence.

At the beginning of the project those who did speak up would tell their stories in an excessive way, 'over-talking' and 'over-describing', as if they desired to cause the listener pain. The men would become highly animated. Unable to sit still, they would jump up and describe in horrific detail how they had been tortured, acting out parts of it for greater effect. They would look at the facilitating team to see our reaction and frequently repeat what they had been saying becoming louder, angrier and more explicit in an attempt to shock or upset us. Part of learning to tell our story is knowing how to tell it. Finding a voice is not so much about speaking up as it is about finding how to use that voice. These men were overcome by silence, partly because when they had tried to tell their stories, they had done so in a way that no listener had found acceptable. The telling of the stories had been directed by their anger and frustration. One of our goals was to not just give a voice but to help the men negotiate their way around their stories and realise that their anger was rarely the driving force behind that voice.

Dealing with so much anger meant finding a way within the project to allow it to be expressed in a constructive manner. It also meant taking the group through exercises to help them realise that they were experiencing a range of emotions beyond anger and that their memories also extended beyond those of their torture and imprisonment. With time, the undercurrent of anger, which was often directed at the facilitating team, came to represent merely a stage in the process. It was more about their need to have their right to feel anger acknowledged than the need to openly express it. For me, it was about finding ways to balance all these areas as and when the need arose.

I planned each session meticulously, but I quickly realised that applied theatre work requires a plan as a guide for moving forward, not as a line of action to be followed unwaveringly. As a participatory project, the group members would be the ones to decide the direction we took. Sometimes this was a result of their own ideas and the issues they wanted or needed to explore; sometimes it was because of issues that arose in the exercises we did and how I guided them in certain directions; and sometimes it was caused by the obstacles they faced personally in exploring what had happened to them. In every case I realised I had to see the patterns which emerged and adapt or change my plan accordingly – on the spot.

With a group so determined to be heard and so angered at the enforced silence imposed on them, I did not expect to be faced with a wall of silence when the workshops began. As individuals they had been very vocal and frustrated at not being listened to, yet when they were finally granted an environment in which they could be heard, their immediate reaction was silence. Finally they had a platform from which to speak, yet many found themselves unable to, or were so overwhelmed by working out where to begin that they resigned them-selves to silence. Original plans of discussing shared experiences had to be quickly abandoned. To help these people find their voices, I first had to strip away any need for them. Image theatre seemed the logical approach, allowing for contemplation and study of intent and comprehension. It serves as the formulation of the concept into a concrete form, enabling memory to build – as described below.

For these men, anger, frustration and a desire for revenge meant they were not looking at what had actually happened to them but were driven by their overriding thoughts and feelings. Most had never worked through what had happened, but instead became fixated on how it had made them feel. This meant that using words to describe what had occurred was difficult for them. Despite their desire to speak and how animated they became when they eventually did so, they were often incoherent, unable to express themselves as the memories tripped over one another. This in part accounted for why they had not been listened to.

It reminded me of how, as a child, I had struggled to express myself because my elder sister would deliberately speak over me. I taught myself to speak incredibly fast in the hope of being heard. The result was that I became incomprehensible to others, even though I could not hear this myself. For a year I attended speech therapy to learn to slow down and lose the fear that I would not be heard unless I spoke at speed. Working with these men reminded me of that. On the few occasions the men had been listened to, they had overloaded their listeners with non-stop inappropriately graphic descriptions of torture. Through image theatre they could build a picture and then manoeuvre around it, piecing together their own impressions.

I asked each man to create his most memorable image from their time in prison. All had been tortured, held in captivity in inhumane conditions often with twelve to eighteen people in one small standard sized cell of 2 by 4.5 metres, for months, even years. Their initial images were not ones I would have expected

- the victim collapsed on the floor during a torture session with a doctor checking his vitals to decide whether or not he could withstand further torture; many later discussed how the person they came to hate most throughout their captivity was this doctor figure who held the power to stop each torture session

- a recurring image created by many of the men consisted of a group squashed together in a cell, laughing at jokes they were telling one another: images of camaraderie were created with meticulous detail each time

- an image of those in the cell listening uncomfortably, some with their hands over their ears, to someone being tortured in another room. Although the torture itself was never depicted, all the men looking on at the created image immediately recognised what was happening

- an image in the cell of the men singing and using their bodies as musical instruments. In this image we saw again laughter and enjoyment

- an image of the prisoners standing under a vent shaft where the rain would come through: some men were trying to drink, while others tried to clean themselves. When I asked the other men what they saw when they looked at this image, three simultaneously shouted out 'dignity'

None of the images representing the men's most memorable moments from their imprisonment depicted torture, and many showed moments of laughter, joy and happiness. While I was surprised, the men were shocked and bemused to discover how many positive memories they had and how prominent these memories were. It was important to explore this to diffuse the anger, to gain perspective on the situation and to rebuild memory more accurately.

The activities the men had used to pass the time in prison became set activities within the workshops. Each time emotions began to run high or anger took over, we would do one of these activities and the men would relax. As these were activities the men had actually carried out, all suggestions came from them. Thus they quickly became part of the creative process of the workshop, contributing to the direction it took. The activities were basic, superficially at least, but they played a key role in forming these men's stories and in finding the voices they were searching for.

The activities they used from their time of captivity included:

- telling one another the funniest joke they could remember, but the condition was always that the joke had to be told expressively and acted out

- creating music from their own bodies and singing, something the men had found empowering particularly because it infuriated the guards and although many remembered being beaten for this, they insisted it had always been worth the risk

- inventing incredible ways to escape their situation, highly creative ideas which often incorporated magic and superheroes

- telling one another stories which were often focused on failed escape attempts which they would embellish and over-dramatise

- impersonating the guards and other officials – again something for which they were frequently beaten yet continued to do, as they considered the beating worth the laughter it created

A few weeks into the project, one of the men said to me, 'It's important that people know how much we laughed, you must tell them that!' The man standing next to him interrupted: 'It's more important we remember. How is it possible we had forgotten the laughter?'

In another image theatre exercise, the men worked in groups to create a single image representative of political imprisonment. Each man in turn stepped out of the image and then adapted it to speak to his personal experience. He was free to move the location of those in the image, take them out even, but not to alter the shape or position they had been allocated in the original image. Finally, when each man was happy with the new image he had created, he inserted himself in a way he considered appropriate. The positions were held for some moments before all returned to the positions of the original image and a new person would step out to create an image representative of his own personal experience in the same way. All this was conducted in silence. There is a Buddhist saying that the mind is like a cup of dirty water; if you do not stir the water, the dirt will settle and the water will become clear. Image theatre works in a similar way. By removing words, clarity is achieved in the concepts vying for a position in our minds.

At the end of the exercise, the men sat in groups and discuss the images they had created, how they differed and how also many of them stemmed from one original concept. The discussion centred around what had occurred in the exercise, their observations and feelings about the images. The intention was not for them to relay their personal experiences from their time in prison. The exercise is intended to unite the group, encouraging recognition of how they are all part of the whole. Their images had striking similarities and it was important that the men saw this for themselves. In their isolation and silence, many of these men had come to feel they were alone in their suffering. Finding common ground and sharing is key to the constructive progression of the workshop.

One of the most unifying elements in this exercise came from the men's choice of characters in their images. While the central image represented imprisonment, the setting and characters around that central image changed in the individual images. There were obvious judgmental figures created in each person's image, who usually turned out to be family members. These figures were usually looking in on the prison situation, not directly a part of it; their presence was more symbolic for the prisoners than real. It was clear that the thoughts, opinions and actions of family members weighed heavily on many of the men. Afterwards, they spoke of the pressure they felt they had been placed under by their families. Some felt judged because they had brought this fate upon themselves, others because they had put their families in danger. Some felt betrayed because of the inherent lack of trust the dictatorship engendered by encouraging family members to report one another and offering them rewards if they did. Others spoke of the judgement that comes from people believing you gave up their names during torture and that you were a coward. The fear of being viewed as a coward was a dominant one which I found necessary to revisit frequently throughout the workshops.

Meeting once a week on weekends for four hours over a period of twelve weeks, we worked predominantly with image theatre. Although words were used, it was usually in the form of a group discussion after an activity, or in the sharing of thoughts and feelings about the work. This period of time was necessary to help the men formulate their stories and remember, as well as to nurture an atmosphere of trust. Initially the men had struggled with words and their anxiety at having only a small window of time to tell their story. This often created a desperate muddle as they tried to put together so much information. Image work enabled the group to slow things down and dispel the sense of time being so limited.

In another image exercise, the men explored perceptions of themselves and their situations. Standing alone in a space, they were to mould themselves into three separate images. The first was an image that represented them before they were arrested and tortured; the second an image that represented them during their period of imprisonment; and a final image that represented how they saw themselves since their release. The images were numbered one to three, and participants were asked to move between the images as the numbers were called out. This helps create familiarity with the images and a sense of progression or regression in how the individual perceives himself. Interestingly, the images that generally portrayed a sense of brokenness were the first or the third, rarely the middle one. In fact the middle images frequently portrayed strength and dignified posturing.

After familiarising themselves with the images, the men were asked to return to their first image. They were instructed to gravitate towards those holding similar positions. They then discussed their images with this group, looking at the similarities that drew them to one another. They then returned to their second image. This time they were asked to think of a sound to accompany the image. Once again they were asked to gravitate to those holding similar positions. This time, as they discussed the similarities, they shared the sound they had chosen to describe that image. This allowed for a natural progression of image to sound and ultimately the final stage in which we would introduce words.

As the men made their third and final image, they were asked to think of a single word to describe it. Once again they were asked to move into groups of similar images and during their discussion they shared their word. The groups who had similar images discussed whether their sounds and words were also the same and if not, why that might be. The lack of congruence that often occurred, with similar images but different sounds and words, opened the door to a discussion about perception. In this exercise the words chosen for the third image were usually representative of frustration and anger. They included: dead, forgotten, ignored, broken, defeated, lost. Slowly we were easing into the stories and, in the process, rebuilding memory.

Being able to deal with sensitive topics through games and laughter is a delicate process. Without care it can be viewed as being dismissive, a playing down of the depth and meaning the issue has and an insult to those involved. Failure to play and laugh is equally destructive, as any group can find a common bond in laughter and it forms a key step in the reflection process. With each group the games chosen reflect the make-up of those involved. In a prison or gang setting I am unlikely to play contact games or games that would make the participants feel they were behaving like children. Working with those who have suffered sexual abuse, I take care to avoid starting with games that involve touch and focus on ones that will build an atmosphere of trust as quickly as possible. With refugees and those who have grown up in civil conflict, the notion of play is often alien and I will spend a good deal of time building up basic play skills.

Many games and exercises became memory aids to help participants process their past. Many were focused on selective memories which imprisoned them, and rendered them unable to see beyond a particular incident. For some of the men this was the moment, for example, when, broken down by the torture, they had given names of others or confessed to crimes they had not committed. Haunted by the shame of it, this memory overshadowed any other they had of their experiences and roused intense self-disgust.

Memory games and exercises were used to demonstrate that no single person has a complete picture of the past. Our memories choose to focus on particular aspects of our experience and this can often be destructive. In the Memory Game, one person sits in the storyteller's chair and begins to give a detailed account of a specific experience, in this instance what it was like to be a political prisoner from the moment of arrest. If any of the others listening thinks the storyteller has omitted any detail, he can stop him, change places and continue with his version until challenged, and so on. As this game developed it became clear that the nature of the topic and the processing involved changed it into an exercise. The intent behind the exercise was not only to induce memory, but to move towards processing it.

The first storyteller began with the night the militia came to arrest him – but was interrupted almost immediately. The man who interrupted, Eduardo, began to talk about how they always knew they were going to be arrested, how they prepared themselves by gathering as much information as possible about what would happen to them after arrest, so that nothing could take them by surprise. He commented that this had been one of the hardest things for him; thinking he knew what to expect, being right, yet realising it all came as a shock regardless. Eduardo claimed that it was here the anger truly begins; anger at yourself for being arrested and anger at your own arrogance to think you can prepare yourself for it. The others agreed reluctantly, all with their eyes fixed on the floor.

As the story progressed, most of the interruptions came when the storyteller showed anger. The interruptions spoke of the camaraderie and laughter. They spoke of how through sharing such a small space every day for months, even years, they got to know one another better than they could ever know their own families, even their wives. A man spoke at length about how they had established their own university. The idea was that each person would teach the others about his own area of expertise or knowledge so they could educate one other and keep their minds sharp. When I first suggested the idea of this game, the men had dismissed it, saying there was nothing much to tell and it was a pointless activity. We spent seven hours just on this one exercise dealing with their imprisonment, the men unwilling to bring it to a close, constantly finding more details, that then led to new interruptions. They laughed, cried, cheered and were animated throughout as they rebuilt their stories. They were surprised not only that they had so much to tell, but that so much of it was positive.

The time spent on an activity varies. With one group I might spend twenty minutes on the Memory Game, with another a full day. When I trained as an educator and facilitator we were always taught to pay attention to our timings. In this approach to applied theatre the group plays a key role in deciding how long to spend on any process. I have had to learn how to constantly juggle timings and to know when to ignore my own estimations. It takes courage and belief in what you are doing to play a game for much longer than what would be considered typical. It is an intuitive decision related to realising you are making progress in a way that works for the group and therefore needs to be nurtured. At the same time, as a facilitator I need to maintain a discipline within the activities and their structure.

Working with torture victims was not an easy process. It took time to build trust in both the team and the methods. It was crucial they saw what they were doing as worthwhile or we could not have made progress. As the project grew so did the team I was working with, drawing on people from a counselling, social work and political theatre background. It was through this rapid growth that I learned the importance of putting together an effective team and developing an awareness of the mentality with which every individual approached the project. Throughout the year in Paraguay we worked with numerous games, exercises and performance approaches. This chapter has allowed for only a brief glimpse into the methods and approach used.

The project was later extended beyond Paraguay, where it took place in Argentina, Chile and Brazil, where other groups worked with it over a period of three to six months. In each instance I consulted and helped initiate the project, bringing with me the lessons I had learned from my experiences in Paraguay. Thereafter, local groups of theatre practitioners, therapists and social workers continued and built on the work.

Working with torturers: eliminating judgement

Working with those involved with the dictatorial regime was in many ways similar to working with the torture victims. They all had a story they wanted to tell; they all felt nobody had listened to their side; they were angry and frustrated. Where they differed significantly was in the calm approach they took to the initial workshops, a defence mechanism of exhibiting an aura of control and authority. They were also more guarded in their participation and more calculated regarding what they were willing to share. Hanging in the air was the question nobody dared ask, 'Why had they committed these atrocities?' Intuitively I felt that if we were to move forward, this was the question I needed to ask. We could not advance before there was an opportunity given for explanation and justification. So I asked it.

Their replies forced me to deal with my own judgement towards those I was working with, a judgement that I wanted to believe did not exist but soon realised was present and that it influenced how I looked at the people seated in front of me. They were all men who had been actively involved in enforcing rule under the dictatorship. The majority had worked in the prisons as guards or torturers. I wanted to believe I had an open mind towards these men but the truth was, despite all my efforts to view their situation otherwise, it seemed very black and white. How could a torturer's actions ever be justified? How could it be anything other than the brutal reality of causing unnecessary horrific mental and physical pain to another human being?

One man, Diego, immediately volunteered a response to my question, appearing almost relieved to have the opportunity to broach the subject. 'Imagine' he said, 'you are asleep one night and suddenly your house is broken into by the military. They tell you that you will work for them and, if you refuse, they will kill your wife and children. You may judge me, but tell me this, what would you have chosen?'

I have never forgotten that moment, how my mind raced through the options and the consequences that accompanied them, knowing that no choice could ever be a good choice. Since that day, I have tried to always remember that I have no right to judge, especially when I don't know the story behind the actions. In my work in prisons for example, I always tell the groups I work with that I am not there to judge them and have no interest in doing so. They are in prison so they have been judged already; my work is about taking them on a journey of exploration and this cannot be achieved through judgement.

Diego's story was typical of many of the others in the room that day, but other explanations were also offered. Some spoke of their support for the politics of the regime and the need to maintain order; others said it had been their job and that they had been following orders; a few said that it was their talent. Some felt anger at being forced into the role by an oppressive regime; others were angered by those who had challenged the regime, thus forcing them to become oppressors; and some felt angry at their actions being misinterpreted, when everything they had done, they claimed, was in the best interests of their country and its people. Multiple views existed around the same issue and disagreement had caused these men to take on the role of oppressors. Like the victims, their current of anger was tangible – only this time it was strongly directed at those victims. Many insisted that they only became who they were because the victims forced them into it. Problems arose with concepts of oppressed and oppressor, right and wrong.

Another problem I found with the group of torturers was that they had no sense of unity. They did not share the same feelings towards the regime and, while many regretted what they had done, many did not. This lack of unity created an atmosphere of suspicion, in a group already paranoid about maintaining their secrecy. The disparity of experiences, reactions and justifications in the group meant finding common ground was essential to unite them – and quickly. While image theatre had seemed the logical starting point with this group, my priority now had to be to unite them, otherwise advancing with even the most basic image work would be impossible. Each of the men felt certain that his story was unique and that he had little or nothing in common with the others. The same group of men who feared judgement from the outside world were constantly passing judgement on one another.

I decided to use a storytelling method often referred to as 'Same and Different'. This method emphasises the similar experiences within a group, through acknowledging the differences. One person tells the story of their experience for approximately one minute. The listeners sit with pen and paper and note down three points that are similar to their own experience, and three points that are different. The next person then tells his story based on the three points of difference he noted, while listeners record six points as before. While all the men have been through similar experiences they are at the same time alienated by their personal journeys, their guilt or lack of it, and their perceptions. This activity helps bring them together and becomes a source of comfort and recognition.

One of the men, Carlos, began telling the story of how he himself had been arrested in the middle of the night. After being questioned and beaten, he was given the choice to work torturing others or remain imprisoned and be tortured himself. When he had finished, Oscar began his story based on the similar and different points. Oscar too had been arrested in the middle of the night, but they had taken his family as well. He had been questioned then released, but his family were kept imprisoned. He was never beaten. The choice he was given was to torture others or else his family would be killed. A third man, Guillermo, explained that he had been the one to make these midnight arrests, until one night he was taken aside and placed in a room for questioning. Guillermo's loyalty to the government was questioned and he was beaten. He was then told he was being promoted to the role of torturing others to prove his loyalty. The similarities and differences emerged with each new story.

I decided we could now proceed with image theatre. Removing words made sense in this instance because of the atmosphere of distrust. Each person chose a particularly memorable incident from their experience and created an image to represent it, using the others in the group. Finally they would place a representative of themselves in the image. I asked them to choose another man to represent them so they could stand back and observe the image and its effect. I asked them what they remembered feeling when they were in the situation they had chosen to depict and to volunteer words which described the various emotions they were experiencing. Words shared included fear, pride, anger, frustration and shame.

I asked the men to insert a person to represent them in the image for each emotion. Thus if a man described himself as feeling fear, anger and frustration, he would insert three sculpted versions of himself in the image, each sculpted in a way that represented one of these emotions. The result was that in the end the image became populated by multiple versions of themselves, depicting a range of emotions they experienced in that moment. We had to create one image at a time, as many needed several people to complete it. Moreover, observing how others created their images was informative and thought provoking for everyone involved. This in turn helped create empathy among the men for one another.

This exercise took a long time. While some of the men had chosen to portray themselves carrying out their job in their function as guard or torturer, most had chosen a family scene which, on the surface, looked insignificant in terms of the range of emotions it might offer. It was only as they started moulding the different statues that the depth behind the images became apparent. The men focused mainly on negative aspects such as feeling guilty, angry, frightened, ashamed or victimised.

The next step was for each of the sculptors to go up to the statues and speak to them briefly, explaining why he thought he was like that, or why he didn't want to be like that. The men overwhelmingly spent their time talking to their 'helpless/victim' self which they all identified as being present. It was here, it emerged, that most of their anger and frustration lay. The men worked in groups so there was no audience to what was happening and this allowed for greater privacy. The facilitating team moved around unobtrusively, ready to move in if a problem arose, but also listening on the outskirts to gain greater knowledge and understanding of those they were working with.

I recall one man in this exercise speaking to his 'ashamed self' about being judged now by the same people who had supported and encouraged his work at that time. He talked about how, when the dictatorship was overthrown, scapegoats had been needed. People like him were easy targets, left to bear the responsibility for the atrocities which had occurred. He pleaded with his statue to understand that he had simply been following orders. The idea of just following orders was one many of the men regularly returned to. They were angry at being judged for this, feeling they had no option at the time and that it was those who had given the orders who should be held accountable.

When I started the project, I made assumptions that the victims were only those who had been tortured. The more I worked with their oppressors, the more I realised that they too saw themselves as victims, having been forced into the role of oppressor either by the regime or by those who had opposed the regime and by so doing created the need for the work they did. There were no simple divisions and it forced me to reconsider the way the workshops would develop with this group. To gain their voices they needed to be given the same level of care, understanding and nurturing as the torture victims. The workshops would not be so different.

What was different was their speed of processing. This group advanced much more quickly, digesting the concepts and moving ahead with them. They approached the work in a manner that was more cerebral than emotional. I realised that this created more issues with the lack of trust within the group, and for the facilitating team. Sometimes the responses felt very calculated; after all these were people who had survived by saying and doing the required thing under the dictatorship, survival tactics that continued into the present. Maintaining trust became a priority, as did incorporating games that didn't allow time for calculating, forcing the men to react more intuitively.

It seemed logical to play the Memory Game with this group, as I had with the torture victims, as a means of getting nearer to the truth; the difference this time being that we played it in reverse. We began with the end of the story, encouraging a challenge for omissions as in the original memory game. This variation is useful for investigating causes as the challenges can help to track down multiple causes for why things happened as they did. We focus on different things when we listen than when we speak and this was apparent in the nature of the interruptions. It also helps show what each individual is hanging on to from the past, his individual mental blocks. Most of the men began with their memories and feelings of being persecuted for having done their job. They spoke of how they went overnight from being considered a loyal citizen and upstanding member of the community, to hiding who they were and what they had done for fear of reprisal. From here they worked back through the fall of the dictatorship to their role under the dictatorship, to what it was that had compelled them to work in this area and finally back to their life beforehand.

The interruptions with this group focused around the describing of emotions. The storytellers tended to be very factual; others would challenge and come in to talk about their pain, anger, regret, and their feelings of being judged. What finally surfaced as a unifying theme for all of them was their fear of now being judged by their families. One of the more outspoken of the men, Felix, commented later that they should have begun at the end of the story by describing what it is like to live every day with the fear that your own children will think you are a monster; that your own family will reject you for what you have done. As he put it, 'the regime is something they learn about in school nowadays, they know nothing of what it meant to live through those years. They know nothing of survival and what lengths a man can go to ... or the depths to which he might sink.'

The men spoke repeatedly of being misunderstood and being unfairly labelled. Comments about labelling were linked to how vulnerable each felt and the weight of this. To process concepts of labelling, I created an exercise that looks at the differences between how we view ourselves and how others view us. The exercise, which I called 'Me, myself and I', is influenced by Augusto Boal's image theatre work.

Working silently in groups of three, one man moulds the other two to represent two contrasting views of himself; how he views himself and how he believes he is viewed by others, although he does not tell the statues which version of himself they represent. When the sculptor is happy with his work, he approaches each statue and gives each three words he feels describes him. When this is complete, he moves to stand behind the two statues. Words that came up frequently included: monster, evil, traitor, misunderstood, fearful, façade, loving and angry. In discussions afterwards many men spoke of how the negative words, especially evil and monster, belonged to the image of how they viewed themselves, while for other men these had been the words they felt others attributed to them.

The statues are now armed with two pieces of information: the shape they have been moulded into and the three words allocated them. At this point the statues gain their voices and create a monologue about who they are. Physically they remain statues, unable to move their bodies throughout the exercise. This prevents the exercise becoming too intimidating for the sculptor. The statues cannot move but they can talk. They all enter into monologues in the first person, inspired by the words and moulding they received. This continues for around five minutes. It is important not to cut the time if they are struggling. In my experience, when they are struggling is when they dig deep and let down their defences. I do remind them that the monologues in our heads are extremely repetitive so that if they run out of things to say, they should start back at the beginning. It is crucial that they never fall silent. If they do, they will begin listening to the other statues and lose their concentration.

When the monologue section is complete, the sculptor stands with his back to the statues. Ensuring that they cannot see him, he places himself in a position indicating how he desires to be and be seen. There are now three statues: how the sculptor views himself, how he believes others see him and the 'ideal'. The sculptor proceeds, still with his back to the statues, to describe the ways he would need to change himself and his life to achieve this ideal. If convinced by what they hear, each statue moves a little to represent how that change would affect their position. When the sculptor finishes speaking the three statues turn to face one another and compare their similarities and differences.

Watching the creation of the statues, I was struck by how similar the images were for all of the men. Those representing how others viewed them were often posed arrogantly, looking down on the world around them. All had wide stances and an air of control as if they were untouchable. Yet in their own views of themselves the statues were often grotesque, hiding their faces and fearful of being seen. When they moulded their ideal image, most took a form that indicated they were trying to explain or justify themselves. Nearly all the statues held their arms open, reaching out. In the group discussion afterwards the men agreed that they had struggled to mention certain things, that they had deliberately avoided other things and had shown an arrogant sense of self-righteousness. Many quickly realised that they learned more about themselves in the role of the statue speaking the monologue for someone else than they did as sculptor. This is because they only have their own knowledge and experience to draw on to realise the image and words provided. And it is one's own experience, opinions and fears that shape each monologue.

Working with torturers presented issues which were more ethical than practical. Many of the facilitating team struggled with what they considered the ethics of working with such people and this created divisions. I found myself frequently passing judgement at first on how I perceived the men. Unlearning to do this required a lot of self-reflection, as did dealing with my own sense of guilt that I liked working with them and enjoyed their company. Everyone we work with shows a reflection of a part of ourselves, but sometimes we simply aren't ready to look in that mirror.

Paraguay: torturer and tortured meet

I felt sick as I waited in the hall, which suddenly seemed too large and for-bidding. Months of workshops first with torture victims and then with torturers were now culminating in this one event that would decide the wisdom of bringing the tortured together with their torturers in a single workshop. It was logical. It made sense in terms of what we had been trying to achieve. But ... and that was the problem: that uneasy 'but' punctuated every thought.

In all my applied theatre work I try to work with the different sides involved in an issue. To understand the issue and the behaviour involved means listening to the stories from every angle. This is not to take a stance on right or wrong. Simply, it helps us, and the people we work with, to gain new perspectives. We are all quick to see every story from our own point of view, quick to judge but slow to listen. I am not suggesting we condone criminal behaviour, or harm caused to another. But simply to dismiss it as wrong, without trying to understand why the behaviour occurred, will never result in future prevention. We need to understand why we do the things we do, why we react as we do, so we can move forward constructively.

After a few months of working with torture victims, I had spoken to them about my approach in working with all those involved in the issue. I explained that this meant I planned also to work with those who had supported and worked for the regime in the prisons, including those who had acted as torturers. They would be in different groups but following a similar process. Had I mentioned this at the outset I am sure the victims would have rejected the idea and the effect would have been detrimental to their own project and their trust in me. Months into the work, perspectives had changed. Some nodded, others shrugged, but they all agreed when I explained my plan. Smiling, they declared categorically that no torturer would come forward to join such a group because that would mean openly admitting the role they had played under the regime. And this, the torture victims assured me, would never happen.

To a certain extent they were correct, but I had already made inroads in this area. My research work had afforded me many opportunities to talk with those who had supported the dictatorships in various ways. And I had quickly learned that they too were eager to tell their stories, that they too had been silenced in their own way. With guarantees of 'eternal' anonymity and protection for their families as well as themselves, I had a group willing to come forward and participate in a sister project.

There were plenty of obstacles and sticky moments during both of the projects. Developing these groups had been challenging as both had been mistrustful, albeit for different reasons. The project had been surrounded by suspicion and I was always the outsider, the foreigner who had not lived through the dictatorship or its immediate aftermath. Every stage of the project had been about facing each challenge head on and looking at how we could somehow move forward. Enough progress had been made with both groups for me to propose an unlikely scenario – that they meet for one session together. In my applied theatre work it is rare that I bring opposing groups together, as it carries unnecessary risks and can be damaging not only to the project but also to the individuals involved. This case I believed to be different.

In these post-dictatorial regimes few had been punished. There were scapegoats who had been tried for crimes against humanity, but the majority had adapted to life under the tenuous democracy which had followed, some even assuming positions within the new government. Most people continued their daily lives as before. This meant that a neighbour, a workmate, even a family member could be someone who had betrayed you. If these people had to live side by side, they needed to find a way for their co-existence to work. Holding on to the anger, the hatred and the fear would never allow that to happen.

A few years later I encountered the same scenario among Rwandan refugees. Tutsis who returned to Rwanda after the genocide found it overwhelmingly difficult living next to their Hutu neighbours. These neighbours were the same people who had played a part in the horrific events of 1994 that left an estimated 20 per cent of the population dead. Many Tutsis had fled to the Democratic Republic of Congo, Burundi, Tanzania and Uganda, as had pro-peace Hutus who had seen their own tribes turn on them for refusing to take part in the massacres. Those who didn't die from disease and starvation in the filth and poverty of the refugee camps went back to Rwanda to rebuild their lives. They quickly found that the events of 1994 had left an indelible mark and that a return to their previous existence was impossible.

In South America there was a subtlety to the betrayal of those who spoke out against the dictatorships. It was a slower process than its African counterpart, engendering a culture of fear and silence over decades. Perhaps for this reason the uneasy co-habitation had been achieved after the dictatorship: it was already embedded in the society during it. These uneasy living arrangements did not remove the feelings that lay beneath the surface. In Paraguay I remember always feeling as though I was living in a pressure pot that could explode at any moment. When it finally did blow in March 1999 the lid was quickly replaced and the simmering continued as if nothing had happened.

Both groups, the torture victims and their torturers, agreed to the single proposed joint session. Their quick agreement took me by surprise. I had expected and been prepared to argue my point with one or both groups. I had prepared lengthy and detailed arguments to support my case. Yet they accepted the suggestion with little or no resistance. Now the moment had arrived I found myself questioning the wisdom of the idea. I was stepping into new territory and that meant facing the possibility that anything could happen. Over the months of listening to the stories from both groups I had been struck by the similarities. Bringing them together to share their work and tell their stories seemed to present a way forward. Now as I watched them enter the hall I was no longer so sure.

The atmosphere was tense and as the men entered they each sought out their comrades and stood with them. By the time everyone had arrived it felt like a scene from *West Side Story*, with rival gangs at opposite sides of the room. Some of the men seemed more uneasy than others and for many of the victims, finding themselves in the same room as someone who had tortured or imprisoned them was clearly difficult. Just as we were about to begin the session one of the men, Julio, who had been imprisoned for four years and endured prolonged torture sessions, looked up and met the eyes of Alberto, the man who had been his torturer. Overwhelmed and enraged, Julio made his way across the room before any of us had a chance to react. He came to an abrupt halt in front of Alberto as if trying and failing to find the words to say to him. When words failed him, the enraged Julio spat in his torturer's face.

The atmosphere in the room became charged. Defences were up, emotions ran high. My heart sank to the pit of my stomach. My mind raced through the possibilities of what I should do next to diffuse the situation. But before I could do anything, Diego, who had been standing with Julio and had spent three years with him in prison sharing not only the same cell but the same torturer, also crossed the room. There was an audible intake of breath from everyone in the hall.

On reaching Alberto, Diego reached into his pocket and took out a handkerchief. With a compassion I had never before witnessed, he wiped Alberto's face clean. Not a word was uttered. Initially stunned, Alberto took the handkerchief from Diego's now outstretched hand and began to sob. Diego placed a hand on his shoulder, then turned to the rest of the room and said: 'Isn't it time we started this workshop?'

For the rest of the day the group worked together. It was tense at moments and some of the men were more willing than others, but everyone stayed and took part in the activities as one group. We chose activities that looked at how they saw themselves in their society, and how they viewed that society. For the most part I asked them to mix when forming smaller groups, which they did with some reluctance at first, but by the end automatically. They were accustomed to the types of exercises and the group work and that familiarity brought them a certain comfort and ease. For one exercise I asked the tortured and torturers to work in separate groups and to create an image that represented something they would like to say to one another. As each group made their image I asked the others to tell me what they saw and what they thought the message was. We didn't seek a correct answer from the group creating the image, as the purpose of the exercise was to look at perception, to look at how multiple readings could exist in one image, and to understand that each person would read it through not just their own experience but also the place they were at on their own journey.

One image created by five of the torturers has stayed with me. Each placed himself apart from the others, almost as if in single images. Two sat with their heads in their hands and the other three took on the positions of the wise monkeys: one had his hands over his mouth, another over his eyes and the third over his ears. When I asked those watching what they saw, they called out: 'guilt', 'shame', 'ignorance', 'defiance', 'pity', 'loneliness'. And then someone said '*trapped*'. There was a moment of silence before it was followed with the words 'imprisoned' and 'victim'. I asked what they thought the message was and one man spoke up: 'the tortured and the torturer is in every one of us – either way were all prisoners'.

Working with performance: playing a role

Some of my applied theatre work consists solely of a series of workshops; a performance is a final outcome of other work; in some projects a production is used as a starting point to introduce the work which will follow; sometimes a performance is used to open and begin an interrogatory process and provoke participants to think about the issue in hand. With this project, the tortured and the torturers agreed that creating a play was the most appropriate way to end. They felt that through a play, they could pursue a better understanding of their own stories and maintain the voice they had struggled to liberate and share with a wider audience.

Applied theatre plays tend to be minimalist in terms of set, props, lights and cast size. My experience suggests that there are two reasons for this. First, the script must be strong and powerful enough not only to capture attention but also to suggest all that is missing. Second, the plays must be easily performed in a variety of locations, rarely theatres, where access to elements such as stage and lights are unlikely. I have performed applied theatre plays in places as diverse as prisons, secure mental units, fields, malls, theatres, schools and universities, garages, shops, buses and streets. Often the space used is so small that the audience is tightly packed around it, making any exit problematic. The sense of feeling trapped can be key to the issue being dealt with, the audience empathising with the story through their own discomfort.

The plays tend to be only one act long. This avoids an interval, which would interrupt the process and can become a safety valve for the audience, or a chance to escape from something that has taken them out of their comfort zone. A final point is that the plays are always accompanied by a talk back session with the audience, giving them the opportunity to question, share, reflect, or simply to exhale. While the scripts are created from the stories released through the projects, I usually take on the role of writer, taking the stories and turning them into plays, and director. The writing is a shared process and stories, or extracts from them, are not used without the consent of those involved.

In the project discussed in this chapter two plays were created. The first, *The Art of Silence* (see appendix), was created from the stories of torture victims and focusing on the story of one man in particular, Emilio Barreto. The second, *The Sin Eater* (see appendix), was created from the stories of the torturers and detailing the reasons they provided to explain their behaviour. Both plays opened in Paraguay, the former in 2005 and the latter one year later. *The Art of Silence* went on to tour in South America, parts of the USA and in the UK. It was also performed at the 2006 Edinburgh Fringe Festival where it was nominated for an Amnesty International Award. *The Sin Eater* was performed in South America, Africa and the UK.

I believe there should always be a purpose behind creating the play and in this project, the goal was to raise awareness, understanding, and to break the silence about what had transpired under the dictatorship. The plays looked at the different sides of the issues: *The Art of Silence* presented the tortured person's perspective and sought to encourage victims to step forward. A committee for human rights had been established in several Latin American countries to award compensation packages to those who had been imprisoned and tortured by the regime. While money cannot buy back the lost years, it can help with medical bills (most torture victims suffer from recurring injuries or permanent damage caused by what was done to them) and basic living costs. But people were not coming forward to claim because of fear and distrust. A play could be used to encourage open discussion and debate on what had occurred under Stroessner. It was hoped that this play would encourage people to come forward and make their claims.

The Art of Silence: a play from the perspective of the tortured

During my work with torture victims the case of Emilio Barreto was brought to my attention. His story came to provide a focus for all the applied theatre work that followed with torture victims in other South American countries (Argentina, Chile and Brazil) and, in some cases, also with those who had worked for the dictatorial regime carrying out atrocities in its name. Barreto's story was striking not only for the horror he had experienced, but also because his story epitomised the experience of so many others. What singled him out was his desperate desire to be heard, evident from the moment I met him. His story became a vehicle to raise awareness about what had transpired under Stroessner, a point of discussion and debate about the past, present and future of the country, an educational tool for the young, and an incentive for others to work through their stories to establish a recorded memory of a time now passed.

On the evening of 22 June 1965 the police broke into Barreto's home, which he shared with his wife of four months, and arrested them both. His wife was released nine months later; Barreto was not released until 15 February 1978. During his thirteen years of imprisonment Barreto was never charged and never stood trial or had recourse to any defence. When I began working with Barreto it had been more than twenty years since his release from prison and his numerous attempts to speak out about what had happened to him had been silenced at every turn, often due to disbelief or unwillingness to believe, or simply because the younger generation wanted to move on and forget the atrocities that clouded their country's past.

The play was written not only as an investigation into what had happened to those imprisoned and tortured, but as a journey into the psyche of a torture victim and the feelings expressed by so many in Barreto's position. Workshops took place over a period of three to six months in Paraguay, Argentina, Chile and Brazil. In these workshops, participants had spoken time and again of their complicit silence. For many this was because they were not being listened to, for others it was about their own unwillingness to confront what had happened to them and what they believed to have been their own inadequacies in such situations.

The Art of Silence is a psychological political drama based on the experience of Barreto. Ten of his thirteen years of imprisonment were spent in a single cell, two and a half metres by four, in which up to eighteen others were imprisoned at times. The play aimed to show, indirectly, the effect of oppression on an individual, the means used to survive and the cost of that survival. The two characters were a young Barreto experiencing the horror of his situation and an older Barreto remembering and at times attempting to communicate with his younger self, who is oblivious to his presence. Although originally based on events in South America, the play follows one person and makes no reference to a particular place and time, so it is applicable to any oppressive situation. The stage set was basic: no scenery or props, and only simple lighting. The actual torture and the other people who were imprisoned are never seen; they are viewed only through the younger Barreto's reaction to what is happening around him.

The goal of the play was to tell Barreto's story and, through his story, to release the stories of others, sparking debate and discussion in the current political and social situation in Paraguay and other countries in South America. I made the complex and questionable decision to allow Barreto to play his older self in the play. This was by no means an easy decision as there were some obvious risks. However a key part of applied theatre is its participatory nature and so it seemed fitting that Barreto, an actor himself, should have this opportunity. What was to follow was fascinating, rewarding at times, disturbing and wearisome at others.

In our first week of rehearsal we discovered that in addition to the already known list of long term injuries and ailments Barreto suffered as a consequence of his torture and incarceration, he had problems with his working memory. Emilio struggled with the mental processes that are used to temporarily store, organise and manipulate information. He therefore found learning lines challenging and this affected rehearsals, the workshopping of the material and his relationship with everyone involved in the production. As we made our way through rehearsals, Barreto would often recall other incidents and, out of a mixture of respect and necessity, we would stop and allow him to relate them. Enabling Emilio to process these memories added hours onto the rehearsals. At times lines of the play created confusion in his mind and he would become uncertain of where he was or whether he was back in prison. We would have to stop and give him time to take in his surroundings and process where he was.

There were times when he became infuriated by his past and would take his anger out on the cast and crew, hurling accusations and insults, incidents of which he would have no memory an hour later, although we were often left nursing our bruises. For his fellow actor, Nelson, the licking of wounds was not always metaphoric. In the play Emilio's character would have flashbacks and at these moments he would take on the role of others involved. For example, in scenes depicting the lead up to torture or a description of the torture, Emilio assumed the role of a guard and each time he did so, he would become excited and throw himself into the role, sometimes losing control and physically attacking Nelson. Each incident was discussed and processed before we continued. The whole process was therapeutic for Emilio, who felt he was dealing with demons he had carried around for years, but it was a strain on everyone else.

On the opening night of the play in Asunción, Paraguay, there was a post-performance discussion with the audience. The audience was made up of others who had been oppressed by the dictatorship: families of victims, supporters of the dictatorship and people who had actively participated in torture and imprisonment, and others who had been directly or indirectly involved in the complicit silence that had engulfed the nation. During that first night's discussion members of the audience stood up one after another and apologised to Barreto for not having listened to him – particularly the journalists he had tried to speak to. Others apologised for the support they had given the dictatorship through their work or through their silence. For Barreto and others like him this was the moment he had waited almost thirty years for, a moment he had lost all hope of ever seeing. Open discussion began about the dictatorship and the need to break silences, and more and more survivors found a way to tell their story at last. The discussion afterwards became a key part of the production, often longer than the play itself and inspiring follow up work and exercises.

When the play went on to tour in the UK and eight other countries with various casts, I wondered how it would be received by an audience alien to the oppressive tactics of a dictatorial regime. What I did not expect was that the play would take on a new life as people related it to their own silence at the hands of oppression. So as the play continued to tour, it became necessary to establish applied theatre workshops to work with the issues that surfaced. Evoked by the audience responses, small applied theatre projects were set up – with rape victims, with ex-military personnel, with groups dealing with issues of bullying, bereavement and asylum. Many of the spin off projects seemed, on the surface at least, to be distant from the original topic, yet the audiences didn't see it that way.

Several ethical issues arose over what the play appeared to be unleashing in those coming to see it. The decision to have Barreto act as himself also raised issues. Barreto explained to audiences, who feared that his reliving his years of imprisonment caused him pain, that each night he performed he felt he was giving away a part of his story and with it a part of his pain. He spoke of being able to educate others but at the same time lighten his own burden by sharing his story and speaking for others like him. Barreto continually told audiences of the release the performances gave him and how he enjoyed participating in the talkbacks. Barreto toured for four months with *The Art of Silence* in universities, schools, theatres and festivals in the UK. This tour was funded principally by donations, an arts grant and the revenue created by the performances themselves. For Barreto, the play was an act of liberation; for the rest of us it was taxing. Barreto faced a number of obstacles in preparing his role, which he alludes to in his statement published alongside the script:

> At first, I would not accept the role when Jennifer proposed that I 'played' myself. It seemed to me absurd and even stupid, because the script narrated my own experiences in prison, my own life... 'How can I act my own life?' I asked myself. 'Who else could do it better?' answered Jennifer... I studied the part. I found it very difficult. It was like doing self-analysis. When my director, Jennifer, had not arrived yet to start rehearsals, and out of respect for the audience, I approached the character in the third person, trying to separate myself from him, but when Jennifer saw the character so far away from my own physical self, she recommended that I 'come back' again. It was then that I had conflicts with my permanent dreams and realities; as in my dreams on three consecutive opportunities – subconsciously I guess – I broke Jennifer's world in the form of a globe into pieces. She was not to blame. It was my dream and me. It was all very difficult. Difficult why? Because each line, each part of the text, were threads of my mind, angels and demons that inhabit my memories. They were difficult to avoid when I was constructing the character, otherwise it would not be a work of art. (Hartley, 2005:76)

Today, Barreto continues to practise theatre, particularly street theatre. He works on his own personalised interpretation of Theatre of the Oppressed, particularly forum work that he takes around the countryside as a means of debate and discussion on social and economic issues in the area. And he is active in community theatre, working with street children and improving the conditions of the peasants in the countryside. He views this as his purpose and direction, where his experiences and his attitude towards them have led him. As he explains:

> For me, what makes me think is my ideology, it makes me a human being, it makes me see nature, the animals, the whole environment, because thanks to our ideas we are human beings who can relate deeply between ourselves and things around us ... and it is this that that I want to teach. Life. Not abstract things ... art must serve to extol the human being, to elevate him ... these are the things that we have to try to teach. To restore once again what it means to be human. (Personal interview with Barreto, 25 August 2004, Asunción)

The Sin Eater: a play from the torturer's perspective

The purpose behind *The Sin Eater*, as with *The Art of Silence*, was to enable people to tell their stories. It was not a judgement on the right or wrong of their actions, nor did it take sides. It merely relayed the stories through a series of interviews. With *The Sin Eater* it was decided to use professional actors and not people who were directly involved, as that would sensationalise the play and could put individuals at risk. Told from the torturer's perspective, the goal was to encourage debate and deeper understanding of a topic many believed to be black and white. As TVO has developed we have sought to look at an issue from as many perspectives as possible and encourage people to question every-thing. After all, there are no simple answers to complex questions and what is needed is open debate and discussion. *The Sin Eater* opened with a contro-versial statement from one of the torturers:

> When people talk of torture all they imagine is the victim – what they must have gone through, how they suffered. Then they talk of the monsters that carried out the torture, what animals they must be, how they lack any sense of humanity, of decency, that they are the stuff that nightmares are made of. But you could be the monster of that nightmare just as easily as you could be the victim. And when the truth is told I, the torturer, I too am a victim ... I was just following orders. (Hartley, 2007:11)

When the play opened in South America the critics were quick to respond, shocked that the same people who had produced *The Art of Silence* could have now produce a play such as this. They talked of us siding with the torturers and questioned the ethics of the project, asking how it was possible to have worked with such evil people. Amid the criticism and the questioning one organisation, a 'society for torture victims', stood strong in defence of the play, speaking out publicly about perception and the need to look at all sides. They spoke of the need to acknowledge that in essence the torturer and the tortured are a part of each of us and that turning a blind eye to one group does not erase their existence, and of the need to hear all stories in order to understand ourselves and others, our behaviour, our choices and our relationships. They pointed to the intertwining of stories separated by that fine distinction created by perspective. *The Sin Eater* has been performed in various countries, showing that torture is as endemic as silence. The play has been found particularly relevant in African nations and been used as a means of looking at tribal division and warfare.

Creating *The Sin Eater* was a different experience from creating *The Art of Silence* and I found it more difficult as writer, director and the workshop facilitator. Initially, I thought the struggle was a result of the subject matter and my own fears that it would be misunderstood and people would be judgmental. As I reread the finished play it became clear that my struggle lay elsewhere. I realised that the character I was reacting to and disliked was not any of the torturers but the interviewer. The play is written as a series of interviews with different torturers and traces the reactions of the interviewer to the responses he receives. My intense dislike for the interviewer sat uncomfortably with me, as this character was basically the role I played in the workshops. It had not occurred to me before that in many ways the plays were as much about us, the facilitators of applied theatre work, as they were about the individuals whose stories we shared. This realisation was disconcerting and disturbing, making me feel almost overwhelmingly self-critical. Each time I looked at the play I had to force myself to treat the interviewer with the same non-judgemental and open-minded approach I applied to those I worked with in the projects. Only in this way did I learn to forgive the naivety, ignorance and judgemental stance inherent in the character of the interviewer and, therefore, in me.

TVO performances are usually accompanied by a talkback. This is a crucial processing and reflection phase for the audience, actors and also for the facilitators involved in the project. New questions are often raised and in answering them, we increase our own understanding of what has often been an intuitive process. The audience's reaction and commentary often gives us deeper insight into the issue being presented. This in turn informs our work as we proceed, enriching it in the process.

Reflections

This was the first major project I had led. I quickly learned that I had made many assumptions, not only about the direction of the project, but also about the people involved. Stepping back and allowing the project to become truly participatory was a frightening prospect. I like being in control and I had to revise what that meant when it came to applied theatre work. I was also starting to learn what my style of work was and my way of processing things as they happened.

Although there was always a plan, it rapidly became clear that the plan would often have to be adapted. Everything that is happening in the moment needs to be observed, to judge what is in the best interests of the group and what would help the participants progress. It is the same process every time an exercise is not developing as hoped. The key, generally, is to have a bank of activities to turn to and being familiar enough with them to bring them rapidly to mind. I realised that as we had progressed through the project, I was also working out how games and exercises could be adapted or new ones created. I would try these out with the group with varying degrees of success and then refine them for future use. The more I worked on the project the more intuitive this process became.

What was frustrating for my co-facilitators was not the changes but my expectations that they were going through the same process. Adapting and being flexible with the plan was something they were all used to and trust was well established within the team. However, their trust was that I would intuitively create these games and exercises and they would adapt to them. My learning process was to see that others needed time to be able to do this, to reflect and think things through. It became key for me always to explain to the team afterwards the changes I made and the new exercises I came up with. This was something I struggled with as I realised I constantly made so many assumptions about what seemed to me to be obvious.

The importance of creating a strong team was the most significant lesson I learned on this project. It is impossible to do this work alone, and everyone in the team brings different strengths to the process. Learning how a team can complement one another, and why their different strengths are needed at different times, required study and planning. In previous projects that I had participated in, my impression had been that the teams were thrown together, often created depending on people's availability. In many cases this was probably true. But when I looked at examples of effective teams, I realised that it was about complementing one another's strengths.

The personal reactions of the team to the groups we were working with caused difficulties. Listening to the torture victims, some of the facilitators became emotional and tearful. Sometimes the stories and experiences are moving, even traumatic to listen to, but the team needs to be able to work with this objectively. After the workshops the team always needs to meet, discuss and work through these issues and how they are feeling, but during the actual sessions they need to step back and be objective and dispassionate. Whenever a team member became openly upset by things they heard, this was in effect taking away the voice of the torture victim. Seeing a facilitator upset, the torture victim often felt he had done something wrong in sharing his story, or felt the need to comfort the facilitator. In these cases I removed the facilitators from the project. This may seem harsh but with issue-based projects the team must be able to deal with whatever that issue is. The group needs to be able to trust the facilitators and feel safe sharing any information. That safety is endangered if the facilitators become overly emotional or make things too personal.

As a facilitator you are constantly gaining new awareness of yourself, your own comfort zone and your limitations. Naturally you try to push yourself and develop more, but there will be times when you are not the best person for a project, or are unable to separate your personal feelings from the work. For me, my struggle with this came when I worked with the torturers and I became aware of my own unintentional but underlying judgement. Had I not been able to work through that, it would have been ethically necessary to excuse myself from the project.

Many of the groups I have worked with are angry and aggressive when we first meet them. Both groups on this project were suspicious, fearful and angry when we began the workshops. It can be difficult to accept that this anger is not about us, even although it is often forcefully directed at us. Time and again on projects I have had to remind myself not to take things personally – the insults, the threats, an initial lack of cooperation. Over time trust develops and the group is regretful of its initial behaviour. I believe it is important that group members are not *made* to feel they should be regretful, as their responses are natural and a part of the process which is being set in motion.

In this project I made the complex and questionable decision to bring the two groups together. This is not something I had previously practised except on very rare occasions, and I have continued to do it only in exceptional circumstances. When working with more than one side of an issue, I believe it can be productive to bring the groups together when those groups have to co-inhabit the same space. In Paraguay some of these people worked together, lived next door to one another, even their children were in some cases friends from school. I felt that not dealing with this could potentially be more destructive than the risks. However I learned how much preparation needed to go into such a meeting, the precautions that needed to be taken and the danger of such an act sensationalising the situation. Because of the risks involved, this uniting of groups, should occur only when it is in the best interests of everyone involved, and never as an experimental move.

The projects in South America were so successful that they continued for several years in the various locations. It would have been easy to get caught up in the success and lose sight of the reason the project began in the first place, allowing the workshops and the touring of the plays to continue indefinitely. Knowing when to stop a project, especially if it seems to be enjoying continued success, can be extremely hard. My fear was that we were beginning to use the same process every time a new group opened so that it risked becoming more a taught process than one influenced and led by the participants. At that point we had reached a stage where we had to decide whether to stop and revisit the applied theatre approach or to proceed with a set programme. To keep true to our belief in what applied theatre should entail, we revisited our approach for each project, treating each one as individual and distinct.

Letting go as a facilitator means handing the project over to others to continue and knowing that it will be adapted and changed, letting go of control over a production and trusting that it will continue to be effective. While letting go is a necessary part of the process, it is one of its most difficult aspects, one I still struggle with on occasion. It is at those times that the feedback and reflection process with the team becomes so important.

Principles and practice

- Work needs to be flexible, to allow the participants to lead the project, while guided and supported by the facilitators
- Always have an action plan that can then be adapted according to the outcome of each stage of the work
- Approach the work in a disciplined yet intuitive way
- Work with a carefully constructed team who can be trusted to adapt to changes quickly and support one another
- Every project is different and should be treated accordingly
- A performance can be used to introduce the project and to develop it
- Be aware of the role of perception and that we all interpret things differently
- Working with those involved in both sides of an issue allows for a more rounded project

- The focus in all projects is on encouraging an understanding of ourselves and others
- Avoid telling people how to behave; explore their behaviour with them
- Avoid talk about right or wrong; explore perceptions of right and wrong
- Applied theatre is a journey and people must therefore be allowed to arrive in their own time
- Image theatre work allows breathing space to help people find their voice and explore ways in which they can use it
- As facilitators we should always use the knowledge and experience of the group we are working with
- At times topics can be dealt with through games and laughter but sensitivity must be employed
- Do not be afraid to let exercises and games go on longer than expected or planned. The best results often come after we begin to feel an activity has gone on too long
- Public performances of issue based plays should be accompanied by a talkback to enable the audience to understand and share in the process. This in turn informs and enriches project work
- When working with more than one side of an issue it can be productive to bring the groups together but this should occur only when it is in the best interests of all parties involved. It should not be an experimental move
- Know when to stop a project because it has run its course or because the team need to step away from it to gain new perspectives
- Incorporate reflection and feedback sessions with the facilitating team after every session

2

Ganglands

We got off the subway and began walking towards the community centre where the workshop was to be held. Rival gangs were gathering for a twelve-week intensive programme to look at alternative approaches to dealing with their differences – alternatives that did not involve shooting or stabbing.

It was in a bad area of town. Here unemployment, teenage pregnancy, gang rapes, drug and alcohol abuse were all part of daily life. The subway station was a twenty-minute walk from the community centre. John, one of the other facilitators, was walking with me and I was grateful for his company. For a start, I have no sense of direction and frequently get lost, and this was not an area you would want to get lost in. The fact that John is black afforded me some protection as for the last few stops on the train and while walking I was the only white face around.

John proposed I play up my Spanish roots (my maternal grandparents are Spanish) and pretend to be Hispanic so I could blend in better, but the resulting hilarity when I tried made us abandon the idea. I could easily pretend to be Spanish, but acting Hispanic in the States was something else completely. John, who was over six foot tall and extremely well built, had grown up in ganglands himself. He knew the area well and moved around it with relative ease. What with my Scottish accent and being female, I probably wouldn't have lasted five minutes without him.

We were feeling pretty positive that we had got the project off the ground. Expected attendance was high, helped of course by the local community and police initiative behind it. Well – that and the lack of options presented to the attendees. Theatre work clearly seemed a soft and easy alternative to the range of community service options and prison time the gang members had been offered. All had police records but so far only for minor offences. Later they boasted that this was because they hadn't been caught, not that they hadn't committed serious crimes.

As we walked, John and I went over our action plan. We knew that the project would be difficult and that making inroads would take time, patience and very thick skins. We laughed and joked about my accent causing problems, about John's past and about the likely reaction when we announced that we were the theatre people. In my experience of working in prisons, or with gangs and at risk youth anywhere in the world I've found that the word 'theatre' is not normally well received. For that reason we often avoid it, finding people are more willing to do the exercises and engage, even take part in stage performances, so long as we don't mention that word.

Suddenly, out of nowhere, we found ourselves surrounded by three young men wearing gang colours, with hoodies pulled over their heads. Within seconds one had me against a wall with a knife at my throat. The other two had forced John to the ground, one with a knee pressed firmly into his back to prevent him from squirming, the other pressing his foot against the side of John's face, pinning him to the ground.

The one holding me up against the wall began shouting demands for me to hand over our phones, watches and any money or jewellery we had. Unfortunately for our assailants, while we may have been naïve in the mechanics of gang wars, we were experienced at working in difficult areas with challenging individuals. We only carried enough cash for a coffee and our transport home, a work phone, and we never wore jewellery. I told my assailant we had nothing except a few dollars, one phone and a cheap watch between us, but they were not convinced. Their demands increased in volume, while John's face was pressed harder into the sidewalk.

I realised only one of them, the one pinning me to the wall, was brandishing a weapon, and it was an unimpressive one at that. It looked like a kitchen knife but one you'd eat your dinner with, not a carving or chopping knife. The other two were using their bodies to hold John, who was considerably larger than either of them, down but they appeared not to have any weapons. Indignation took over. I was not about to be attacked and robbed by three teenagers who could only scrape up one kitchen knife among them! This was clearly a crime of opportunity, driven probably by boredom more than any real desire to inflict injury. So I decided to take a stance and refused to hand anything over. In retrospect, I can see that perhaps fear caused me to react so recklessly and in a way I would not recommend to others in a similar situation.

John looked at me as best he could with a foot crushing his face, in what I suspect may have been bemusement and horror, and began shouting at me in a muffled voice.

> John: What the f***? Jennifer give them your phone and money.

> Me: No! They're pathetic. They only have one stupid knife. I'm not giving them anything!

> John: Give them the f***** money!

> Me: No.

I couldn't help but notice the irony in the fact that John was making more effort to get me to hand over the money than our assailants were. They were now looking at one another in confusion. John and I continued with what became a heated exchange over some minutes, escalating in volume by the second until finally one of our hoodied assailants intervened:

> Hoodied youth: Shut the f*** up lady, this 'aint worth havin' to listen to you! You can keep your f***** money. Crazy f***** bitch!

Deciding we were clearly not worth the bother, they muttered a few threats about finding us later, and ran off. John scraped himself off the ground, glaring furiously at me but steadfastly silent as he motioned for us to continue walking. After a couple of minutes he finally exploded, graphically pointing out all that could have happened to us. Suitably scolded, I agreed that we'd draw a line under the event. We continued on our way, bruised in more ways than one, but determined not to let it affect the project or our attitude to the people we were about to start work with.

The community centre was a large dingy building, paint peeling from the walls. It was easily spotted thanks to its vandalised exterior and the huddled groups smoking something outside, who all looked at us threateningly as we went in. As it neared the time to begin, we gathered in an old style hall with an elevated stage platform on which chairs had been placed. John and I were asked to sit on the last two available seats at the far end of the stage, alongside the others responsible for the series of projects that were to form part of this initiative.

We took our seats and looked out at the fifty plus faces in front of us, none of whom seemed impressed or in the least happy to be there. Most sat sprawled out in their seats, with their legs wide open in a territorial and defiant posture. The room was clearly divided according to the gang colours they had been warned not to wear. Enforcing rules was clearly going not going to be easy.

That was when we noticed, sitting in the first three seats on the second row to the left, our three assailants. These were to be our students for the next twelve weeks.

Background

Gang violence is widespread in the US and all fifty states have come up with innovative ideas to try to tackle the problem since the mid-20th century when it began to escalate. These programmes have sought to establish a framework for intervention and prevention and have had varying levels of success. A few years ago one locality took the brave decision to implement an arts programme to look at gang behaviour and work towards prevention through giving youths greater understanding of the risks of involvement in gangs and the possible alternatives that exist. I was invited to help lead the theatre programme.

At the time I was working mainly on projects related to my work with torture victims. Like the other people I worked with, I had my own professional work – I was a university lecturer, and then went on to work as an education manager. We gave up our free time and received little or no payment for the work we did on these projects. Any grant money or funds raised were explicitly for making the project happen, not for paying the facilitators. As more and more projects arose, we had discussed the need for us to formalise our activities. More work kept coming in and we needed to start looking for formal ways to pursue the projects we wanted to do. We had begun discussing the possibility of becoming a registered UK charity and what that would mean for all those involved in terms of workload demands. Meanwhile I found I was being asked to collaborate and contribute on more and more projects around the world and to design issue-based workshops using applied theatre methodology to work with a range of problems and groups. My full time job was starting to get in the way, but it was where I earned my living.

I had recently been asked to contribute to an artistic approach to gang violence, working with 16-22 year-olds. Each team on the programme consisted of professionals in a particular art form – various visual arts, music, film and theatre – who were experienced youth and social workers accustomed to working with gangs and police representatives. There was a conspicuous and non-negotiable police presence in case of emergencies. With rival gangs on the programme, emergencies became the norm and the facilitators quickly learned that there was no art implement or musical instrument that could not be transformed into a weapon with lightning speed and remarkable creativity. The film equipment all went missing within the first twenty-four hours, effectively closing down the film programme. My general rule for equipment in gang and prison workshops is that if you can't screw it down, you don't have it in the room. After the attempted mugging at knifepoint en route to the workshop, I made it clear to the organisers that we would be approaching theatre in a minimalistic fashion and so not even chairs would be allowed in the room at first. I have learned from years of doing workshops with volatile groups, that if something is not bolted to the ground or walls, it can be turned into a weapon in the blink of an eye.

There would be three of us in the theatre team, two local Americans and myself. I had worked with John and Ian, both social workers with training in applied theatre approaches, on other projects in the US and Central America. Both had considerable experience working with gang related issues and had asked me to join them to help shape a suitable programme using applied theatre. They felt it would be valuable for there to be a woman on the facilitating team. The groups we were working with were all male, repeat offenders of minor offences, who had been placed on this opt-in programme – an alternative to a stint in jail. But from the outset, I got the distinct feeling few, if any, had been given the choice to opt out. Rival gang members had no desire to work with one another and the atmosphere was threatening. The feeling was tangible that violence could erupt at any moment.

The participants were broken down into smaller groups which would rotate between sessions with the different arts subjects throughout each week. By the end of the first week the film programme had been shut down, as had sections of the music and arts programmes. The youths were divided into three groups of 15-20 and we saw them for an average of eight hours a week, spread over a twelve-week period. None of the gang members were thrilled at the idea of attending drama sessions and wasted no time vocalising their discontent and their opinions regarding the kind of people they felt became involved with theatre. John and Ian, both from gang backgrounds themselves and heavily into sports and weight training, challenged the stereotype the gangs were expecting from a theatre workshop. I was an anomaly for them and they weren't sure what to make of me. Unfortunately, word had also spread fast that I was 'a crazy mother f*****' after the attempted knifepoint mugging. What's more, I had a strange accent and used expressions that were totally incomprehensible. I was also the only female on any of the programmes.

Despite this I quickly gained respect and a reputation for being tough because I never reacted to the frequent mutterings of the numbers 187 and 023 during the initial meetings. My non-reaction was a result of ignorance rather than toughness, and I was somewhat disturbed to later discover that 187 is the police code for murder, while 023 is a signal to watch your back. Basically, in other words, I had been getting non-stop death threats. I decided not to inform anyone of my ignorance and instead nurture my newly found, though somewhat tenuous, tough image. Every so often, as the weeks progressed, I advanced to the new number of 51-50 being muttered in my presence. I comforted myself that at least they were no longer whispering veiled murder threats with their digits, until I discovered that this is the code for a mental patient or crazy person. John informed me of this in between guffaws, after he discovered that Ian had thought they were trying to guess my age!

During the official opening when I had realised our attackers were sitting in front of us, an avalanche of thoughts had hit me. My initial reaction was anger, mixed with fear and a sense of foreboding. As we sat there staring one other out, I suddenly found myself smiling, which was definitely not the reaction they expected and added to their confusion and their belief that I might be insane. John, accustomed to working in that area with gang violence, remained angrier with me than the guys who had attacked us, although he did try to deny this. He had not minced his words about my stupidity in arguing with the attackers and refusing to hand over the money. Of course he was correct and a few weeks later this was confirmed when our attackers told us that, had they not been en route to the workshops, they would have been carrying guns and I would most certainly be dead. I would like to believe that had they been carrying guns, I would have shut my mouth and handed over the money.

As I smiled at the three assailants, my thoughts were on how best to handle the situation. If we reported it, the programme would be in jeopardy before it even began, we would never be able to establish trust and we would be more aligned with the police than we already were in the eyes of the gangs. In these kinds of workshops, just as in prisons, I find myself walking a fine line. If we are seen as an extension of the police or penal service, we will get nowhere. If we do not establish our authority, however, we will be walked all over and risk putting ourselves in harm's way.

When we were allocated our first group, the police representatives accompanied us to conduct the initial introductions. We were informed that this was the plan – not consulted. The police officer asked each gang member to say who he was and something about his gang career to date. When it came the turn of our first attacker, it was clear he was waiting for us to inform on him to the police. As he began, I interrupted, 'I think we've already met'. He stared at me and the tension increased dramatically. 'I think we bumped into you and a couple of your friends on the way here.' The guy, who went by the unique name of 'Uh-Huh', stared at me defiantly, waiting for me to snitch on him. I had no intention of doing so, but equally it had to be established that I knew who he was and what he had done, that I had the power to give him away and was choosing not to. In time I would deal with what had happened, but first I had to find a way to make this group respect, work with and trust us.

The introductions presented our first difficulty – the names. All the participants had been told not to wear gang colours or use their gang nicknames and had flagrantly ignored both rules. They introduced themselves with names such as Blood Messiah, Machine Gun, Mad Dog, The Grim Reaper, The High Executioner and Organ Grinder. By the time Organ Grinder had spoken, I was starting to feel thoroughly inadequate at the prospect of introducing myself as Jennifer, and my mind was wandering through possible alternatives that made me sound more threatening. I was sure, based on the gestures that accompanied Organ Grinder's introduction which were aimed mainly at me, that he was not referring to musical organs with accompanying monkeys, but the vital ones inside my body. The police had evidently had enough:

Cop: Enough with the nicknames asshole!

Organ Grinder: What tha dilly yo? That aint no nickname!

Cop: Wot, you tellin' me your bo janglin' momma christened you Organ Grinder?

Organ Grinder: Word up! You makin' a fool of ma momma 5-0?

The gang members started jeering and clapping, jumping at the opportunity for confrontation. John and I exchanged a glance and knew we had to step in. The gangs were looking for a reason to provoke and the police, already dubious about the programme, were looking for a reason to shut it down. The anger and distrust was destroying any chance of progression. Our agreement with the police was that their presence would be unobtrusive, and they would not interfere unless violence erupted. John politely invited them to move to the back of the room, escorting them so he could subtly remind them of our agreement, while Ian and I gathered the group into a reluctant circle.

I wasn't feeling too hopeful about our chances of implementing any kind of theatre project and a small voice inside my head was telling me to run, a voice that was gaining conviction by the second. We had only been in the room fifteen minutes and already it felt like hours. The only way forward was to address the blatant unwillingness of the young men to participate in the programme and the reasons that lay behind it. Letting the gangs vent would get it out in the open and give us some clues about how to approach the group through theatre. So I asked them why they were angry about being there – and opened the floodgates to thirty minutes of ranting fury.

In the most colourful and expressive language imaginable, they criticised the penal system, the police, one another, us, our inability to understand their lives and what they came from. They ranted about how they would prefer to have been sent to prison than be made take part in some 'arty rehabilitation s*** for gays'. For thirty minutes we sat and listened without interrupting or judging, until they were spent and could think of nothing more to say. Then it was our turn and we deliberately turned much of what had been said around. The key was to pick up what they had said and play it back on them, and establish that we too weren't thrilled about being there. Coming in as if this programme existed to save them, trying to sell our programme, or give the impression that we had all the answers, would have alienated them. We made it clear that we all had to work this out together if we were to get through the next few weeks. They didn't trust us and we didn't trust them, and acknowledging that established we had something in common. This was the first step towards building that missing trust.

As the gangs spoke, they harped on about the lies they had been told and the way the police, social workers and facilitators say one thing when they usually mean another. This was important to pick up on, so I proposed an exercise of saying what we heard from one another and what we actually believed it meant. This allowed us also to broach the fact that we were not speaking the same language thanks to the gangspeak and frequent cursing that punctuated their speech. The game was slow to start, as I expected, but quickly picked up pace and as it developed it became a very funny icebreaker.

In this game, entitled 'He/she said, but he/she meant', the participants select comments that have been made and go on to interpret them. The facilitating team get to do the same with the group's comments. For example, when it was said, 'You have been invited to participate in this innovative programme', according to the gangs we meant they were participating whether they liked it or not. When we said, 'we are happy to be working with you on this', we apparently meant that the only reason we were there was because we were getting paid for it. Most of the exchanges were unrepeatable and most spoke to the corruption they believed the penal system to be imbued with. What made some of the exchanges so funny was the translation of what we had said into gangspeak, and our attempts to translate their gangspeak into comprehensible English. John and Ian had more experience with this but with acronyms, abbreviations and number codes, I generally had no idea what they were saying in the early meetings, although that may have been a blessing in disguise.

Body language was usually my main guide to interpreting the group's comments. My inability to understand gangspeak, combined with my Scottish accent, quickly became a source of entertainment and I used this to my advantage. They loved hearing me try to use their gangspeak and were keen to teach me, though I suspect for all the wrong reasons, which made me grateful that John and Ian were there to keep me right. Our willingness to incorporate gangspeak into our workshops rather than ignore or ban it also helped prevent our being viewed as one with the authorities. We weren't with the gangs, but we weren't with the police either and that non-affiliation to either side was necessary to fight pre-conceptions about the work we were doing.

One of the goals the organisers of the project set us was to have a final product from each of their classes – a piece of art, a piece of music, and a performance of sorts. The idea of acting was horrifying enough to the group, but thinking they had to do a performance in front of any kind of public made matters worse. It was clear we had to do two things. First we had to remove any words that associated us with drama and theatre, as they were loaded terms for the group and to attempt to unload them at this stage would have served no purpose. Second we had to establish a baseline to work from, incorporating the things they enjoyed and thus placing them in their comfort zone. This would include things like music, dance, basketball, their personal image in terms of how they dressed and did their hair. It also meant dealing openly and non judgementally with the issues that had got most of them into a gang in the first place, such as drugs, violence and abuse at home, alcohol, street survival, dropping out of school, the need to feel a part of a family and a feeling that they had no other options.

In order to proceed, I asked the group that we agree on some rules for the workshop, rules they, not we would write. This makes it easier to hold them accountable and to build mutual respect. Of course it also meant having to accept their concept of rules. We, the facilitating team, got to participate in this and propose some rules of our own, although even our rules must be proposed through a democratic process and not enforced. Fortunately, some basic rules such as no weapons or cell phones were taken care of thanks to the police security and metal detectors the gangs had to go through at the entrance to the building. I have not always been so fortunate when running gang workshops and have been forced to create game-like activities at the outset to help detect who had hidden weapons, before having them effectively and semi-peacefully removed.

The rules created by the group were basic but significant. They included a strong desire for the police to stay out of the workshops, but the group accepted we had no real power over this. We could, however, insist the police sit at the back of the room and have no participatory role and keep their often derogatory comments to themselves. The group also wanted to be free to use gangspeak, which we agreed to as long as it wasn't being used to disrespect the facilitating team or other participants, or to make veiled threats. The group felt strongly, and rightly, that the way they spoke was part of their identity, so in the first weeks we looked closely at how we could integrate their language into how we worked. We also challenged them to create gangspeak to replace the theatre terms we used, even down to the names for the exercises and games. Our agreement was that as long as it was kept relatively clean, we would adopt the terms. This not only helped build trust, it also created a private understanding of how we all engaged with the work – that it was not being controlled by the authorities. And it showed our willingness to be laughed at. John and Ian, both Americans from gang backgrounds, could get away with using a lot of the terminology. For me, female, white and Scottish, this exercise had a very different effect.

The gang members struggled with making connections between their past and present. This created problems within the project when we attempted to look at patterns of behaviour and the reasons behind not only joining a gang but also carrying out the crimes they committed as a member. To try to establish these connections I suggested that each person brought in something to the next workshop to represent the difficulties of their home life as a child. At the next meeting we had a range of objects and photos. Someone brought in a belt his father used to beat him with; most brought photos of family members lost to drugs or gang violence; someone came with a box of matches;

another brought an old school book; another came with a pair of shoe laces tied in a knot. Where the objects would have been something confiscated as they were searched arriving at the workshop, I had proposed they bring a photo instead. We had photos of knives, guns, syringes, even a fork.

Each object was stuck at one end of a blank wall we were permitted to use. A point was established in the middle of the wall to represent each person in the present as a member of a gang. Over the next week each person's job was to map how that difficulty he had identified in his life as a child led to something else, and that to another thing, and so on until we reached the stage when he joined a gang. We didn't discuss the items at this point, and it was the responsibility of each person to build his journey each day he attended the workshop, mapping it out of actions and consequences in what was to become a mural of their lives. At each stage they could map their journey with a new object, a drawing, a word, or even connect to another person's object if appropriate. At times this was achieved through an exercise, but at others they used the freedom to approach the wall at any time and add to their journey. This allowed them to reveal things they might not otherwise have done.

One day someone wrote in graffiti at the top of the mural '*mi vida loca*'. The Spanish term, meaning 'my crazy life' is often used by gangs to represent their lifestyle. It refers to the notion that the gang motto is to live for now and not think or worry about consequences. The mural had made it impossible to ignore the consequences of their actions, or the connections that had led to them. Similarly there is a common gang tattoo which depicts a smiling and a frowning face to represent the motto 'smile now, cry later'. This was frequently drawn on the mural at the start, but as we drew near the end the smiling face had been removed and someone had written 'cry now'.

The goal was to help bring about recognition of the connections among a group who believed their lives were about isolated events which had no bearing on one another. I didn't ask them to speak about it during these initial stages, because it would have made them self-conscious or even defensive. It was also about anonymity. Information being placed on the mural often involved criminal activity and they needed to trust that this was not being judged or noted down. As members of gangs, image was extremely important and we needed to respect that always, whatever activities we asked them to participate in. This did not mean we couldn't experiment and push them beyond their comfort zones, but we had to do so with care and in stages.

Once the mapping out of this stage of their journey was complete on the mural, we moved to looking at the consequences of being a gang member.

Each individual goes through an initiation process into a gang which can consist of anything from taking drugs, committing a robbery, to stabbing or shooting someone. I asked each of them to begin building a new path on their journey that would commence with an object or picture to represent their initiation into the gang and what they had done. Another week was spent building the journey as gang members. Here actions and consequences became linked to people who had died, or events such as time spent in prison, dropping out of school, acts of violence, and drug taking. We always had to be careful about what was being discussed openly for fear of retaliation among the different gangs at a later stage. With the exercises we were often attempting to find a way for the participants to anonymously acknowledge actions and crimes committed.

For example we played a simple game called 'Change!' Everyone is seated on chairs in a circle except one person who remains standing in the middle. This person would complete a sentence which began with 'I think/believe/feel/ regret...' with a statement about his life in a gang, things he had done and the rationale behind it. After hearing the statement, anyone who agreed it was true for them too would change chairs, while the person who had made the statement would try to sit down on one of the freed up seats. A new person would thus end up in the middle and another statement would be made. As the game progressed the statements became more revealing and people would want to explain the nature of their agreement or disagreement. This made it easy to move into discussion work as the group were open and willing to discuss what had come up. Initially the change of chairs was carried out with an image conscious swagger, but as the game proceeded the swagger was replaced by a desperate dash to get a chair. It was competitive but controlled. It was also a game only introduced at a stage when the group had advanced and were accustomed to working together.

Statements in the game included:

- I think I would never have joined a gang if my mother hadn't been a crackhead
- I believe my gang are the only true family I've got
- I feel I had no choice in doing what I've done
- I regret hurting some of the people I've hurt
- I regret doing drugs
- I think it's kill or be killed on the street
- I believe being in a gang is in my blood

At the start of the third week I asked each person to place something at the far end of the wall to represent where they believed their journey was leading. They were asked to take time to follow the journey of their life as they had mapped it out before they did so. The end journeys for the majority represented prison or death, sometimes both. I remember looking at the end point in the mural and finding it almost overwhelmingly sad. Not one person had shown hope for the future, not one believed their future could offer anything other than prison or a violent death.

With the journey complete, I asked the group to place one final object or image or word in front of the point where their journey began which would represent the dreams they had for themselves when they were young children. The final wall was impressive to look at and the group had taken great care in its creation and been remarkably respectful towards one another's work. They understood one another's journeys totally, no matter how coded or obscure the things they had placed on the wall appeared to us. One man had a picture of his dead brother to mark his decision to join a gang. His brother had been a gang member and had been killed in gang violence. Somebody else had simply placed an arrow from one part of his journey to this same photo to mark what he had done to gain initiation into a gang and had written underneath the word 'sorry'.

The mural became a launching point for numerous other activities and discussions, helping to establish a new openness. Within the group discussions many commented that they realised their stories shared so many similarities, even when they were in rival gangs, and they had not expected that. They weren't completely comfortable with this realisation, but the fact that they stated it openly was a huge step forward. One man even said that the only thing that separated them was the gang colours they wore – and the others nodded in agreement. That same comment made a few weeks earlier would have provoked a violent outburst.

We looked at how we could turn the stories on the mural into a performance. The group insisted that the mural be the backdrop to any performance as it said much more than they could ever say as individuals. They then discussed the two things that had affected them most – their initial identification of the incident from their childhood that set things in motion, and their final piece showing the future. One man remarked that if others could learn to recognise those childhood incidents then they might not join a gang. This was a major turning point. He suggested that if they could show this link through their own stories in a performance to younger people, it might stop them ending up in gangs. I was surprised at the agreement around the room. The performance had not been intended for public viewing, nor had it been requested that it be about not joining a gang. This direction was one the group were taking for themselves. It was a massive turn around for a group who had cursed me repeatedly in the first week when they discovered they would have to do some kind of performance.

Not all the men were eager to perform, but all were keen to be involved in creating the performance and the production of it. In the end they created a narrative talking-heads style piece. This mainly consisted of one person talking directly to the audience about a particular aspect of his story. At certain points he would stop and the others would create images depicting that part of the story, as if in a series of photographs. This enabled them to lead up to an event but to let the image speak part of the outcome as they sat in silence. This was used to avoid admitting or elaborating on certain crimes. The aspect of their journeys they generally focused on were single moments that had produced a chain reaction, leaving them entrenched in gang life: the point as they saw it of no return. Through the telling of their various stories many acknowledged that they could have chosen so many other actions at certain points that would have avoided reaching that point of no return. Some chose to sit centre stage and at turning points in their stories show the path they had taken and the path they could have taken on either side. Discussions with audiences afterwards often returned to this idea and what options might still be available to these young men.

At various stages a narrator, speaking in a freestyle manner using gangspeak, would relate how they were presented with choices and how the choice each made was what led them deeper into the gang world and finally to their death. This was heightened by the fact that during the twelve-week programme we lost some members of the group to gang violence. The men talked about this through rap in the performance.

After the programme was complete, a smaller group committed to working with John to take the performance into local high schools. They performed and afterwards discussed their personal experiences with the students and offered advice. The impact of this was all the stronger because at this stage they had not all left the gangs they were in (many never did) and they talked about how leaving was no easy process. Many spoke less about their fear of trying to get out of their gang, which could cost them their lives, than about their dilemma over not wanting to leave their 'family' although they didn't want much of what being a member of that family meant.

A feedback session had been set up as closure of the twelve-week project. The gangs were invited to present their feedback on the project to the facilitators, in a style of their choosing. Most opted simply to speak about the experience and how transformative they had found it. A few depicted their feedback through graffiti art, even keeping their work within the allocated spaces! Some freestyled (the improvisation on the spot of rap style lyrics, usually performed *a cappella*) and rapped about the ups and downs they had experienced over the weeks and their feelings towards the facilitating teams. Others improvised scenes depicting elements of the process they had undertaken.

Finally a small group, which included our three would-be attackers from the first day of the project, set up a skit situated on a bus. The passengers sat on the bus, some listening to music, while some slept and others engaged in conversation. It became clear that some of these passengers were intended to depict the team, particularly the one playing a woman with a dreadful attempt at a Scottish accent! Suddenly, a gun wielding gang member jumps on the bus and demands that everyone hand over their money, phones and jewellery. The terrified passengers immediately do so, apart from the one portraying me, who begins to lecture the gunman. As they engage in heated dialogue, initially centring on the fact that they can't understand one another, a passenger interrupts, telling the crazy Scottish passenger to shut up and hand over her money. This enrages her further and she begins lecturing him as well as the gunman, who is getting more and more frustrated and waving his gun around erratically. Finally the gunman screams at the passengers to shut up, exclaims that he can't take any more of listening to this mad woman, and shoots himself.

The skit caused great hilarity among both the gangs and the facilitators, especially with its unexpected ending. As the group applauded, however, they turned to face us, applauding us instead of the actors. The skit was their apology for what had happened on that first day. We were never going to get a direct apology, but a relationship had been established and the message was clear to all. With this group, image was hugely important and they needed to find a way to comment and thank us without doing so directly, which would not have been 'cool'. The skit was both a thank you and a means to draw a line under the attack.

As we left that day one of the gang leaders who had been stoically silent throughout most of the project activities approached us. 'You're safe on our streets. Word's out. Nobody touches you.' We looked at one another, not sure whether to feel relived, flattered, or deeply disturbed.

Reflections

Working with gangs and in prison situations underlines the need to have an effective working team. The workshops move at a fast pace. Plans must be changed constantly to adapt to the responses of the participants, but also to prevent provoking or escalating violence and internal unrest among them. Nor can we afford to stick with an original plan that is no longer the best fit for the situation. There is no time to take a break, rethink and discuss the plan with the members of your team each time this arises. With no time to discuss, you have to trust the team to move with you, to understand why a planned activity has changed and to be able to step into the new one without warning. To establish that level of trust and flexibility in working together takes time.

In another workshop where I joined a facilitating team who had never worked together before, members questioned changes to the workshop plan as they were happening and made their discomfort obvious. The participants read this as poor organisation and a lack of unity within the team. If this happens, the discordance becomes the focus of the workshop, and the needs of the participants are pushed into the background. My experience with that team alerted me to how important it is for the team to be able to work well together instinctively. That does not mean the team can never disagree, but we know the time to deal with disagreements or misunderstandings is during reflection meetings, not during the workshop.

In all projects I require the team I work with to have a reflection meeting after every workshop to discuss methods and approach. We know how to work with one another in the moment and we usually understand why an activity needed to be changed or adapted. Understanding what the activity/exercise/ game was changed or adapted into and why this was a better option is part of the team learning process. As we develop this understanding, the team are better prepared for each new workshop.

Reflection time also enables us to let off steam, whether it's about the group we're working with or the people who have commissioned the project, or even each other. Making time and space available for this to happen forestalls any build-up of tension. Any uncomfortable atmosphere can be cleared and we learn to accept constructive criticism, difficult as that can be. It is an essential part of doing this kind of work. Reflection meetings also allow time for the facilitators to discuss their own vulnerabilities and fears. Over the years I have learned to brush off the threats, sexual comments and aggression we often encounter. Working with new members in the team I tend to forget that that is not so easy for newcomers and that not everyone will be able to adapt.

Creating the facilitating team is about looking for a 'best fit', for who will work best in that situation, who will make up the best team for the group we will be working with. There are times when initial aggression and threats can catch me out, or the task ahead seems impossible at the start of a project because the group appears uncooperative. Reflection meetings and being able to sound one another out about doubts and fears becomes invaluable.

John, Ian and I had worked together several times, mostly in challenging situations. We each had different strengths and knew how to use them to complement one another in the workshops. I knew they had greater familiarity with the gangs; they understood their language and where they were coming from. They, in turn, trusted me to develop and adjust the workshops according to the way they developed. But this did not stop John making his thoughts on my stupidity in resisting our would-be attackers en route to the workshop very clear. My standing up to them had placed both our lives in danger.

Accepting my own poor judgement was not easy. I knew I had been wrong. The problem lay in admitting that I had reacted from fear and a determination to prove myself, which would put everyone at risk if carried into the workshop. Learning that it was okay to admit that a project made me feel apprehensive, even fearful, did not come easily. I am often the only female on the projects I have worked on involving potentially dangerous groups. Initial reactions to me are usually in the form of coarse sexual comments and suggestions. When I first started out, I felt I was constantly trying to establish and prove myself in a man's world so I would forget I was a part of a team. I was also failing to trust the work and my ability to use it. Years later my work is still predominantly with males – both the groups I work with and the facilitating teams. I know the sexual comments are a means to test me, my reactions and comfort level. When the comments receive no reaction, they die down and I can be accepted as a facilitator, not relegated to merely a female.

Knowing how and when to acknowledge significant incidents is necessary to the successful building of a project. John and I made a choice to deal with the attack subtly, through the workshop activities that looked at actions and reactions, at alternatives to the violent behaviour patterns the group had learned from being in a gang. Reporting the incident would have jeopardised the project. And the incident had occurred outside the confines of the project and before it began. The group would have felt betrayed had we reported the hold-up but the incident was not ignored. That would have weakened our position and destroyed any hope of gaining their respect. As facilitators we constantly walk a fine line, both a part of the group and distinct from it, rather like Boal's concept of the 'joker' role. Our job is to facilitate and guide, not preach nor teach. At the same time the health and safety of the team must be protected and never knowingly placed in jeopardy.

Another valuable lesson I learned is the power of language and terminology. Terms such as 'theatre' and 'drama' are loaded with preconceptions for many of the groups I work with. Moreover, many of those participating would have their reputation undermined, with potentially serious consequences, were it publicly known they were doing theatre. There are many ways around this, such as simply avoiding loaded words or using acronyms in their place. In this instance the use of acronyms became an inside joke. The group's gangspeak was full of acronyms which I spent a long time trying, with mixed success, to understand. As we began replacing our workshop terminology with acronyms and their own gangspeak terms, the participants became amused and more willing to join in. They also felt they had more ownership of the project. Using gangspeak was provocative in itself as the different gangs have their own terminology for certain things. So each term had to be carefully discussed and agreed upon – for example:

- 602 is a number we used if the group objected to or didn't like an exercise we proposed. At first they spent far too long complaining, but then it was agreed they would call out '602', the number of a prison inmate appeal form, followed by a one sentence appeal as to why we should scrap or change the exercise. In the beginning it was a number I heard a little too often

- The word 'issue' is gangspeak for crime. So asking someone what their issue is equals asking what crime they committed. This caused endless hours of misunderstandings and entertainment

- The group renamed a game we played called Drop Dead 'Poppin and Droppin'. Instead of simply collapsing to the floor if their number was called, they delighted in acting as if they had been shot. The game, like many others adapted, incorporated the violence the gangs were used to. We were not trying to glorify or trivialise the violence but rather to acknowledge the reality of the participants. Pretending it did not exist was not viable because we were exploring their behaviour. It also highlighted the child in all of us and how even these otherwise tough and dangerous men enjoyed playing like children, as we all do

- Near the end of the project we developed an exercise with the group called 'Courting Out'. This is their term for an initiation to get out of a gang. The exercise looked at what kind of things they might have to go through if they tried to leave the gang officially, which is hugely difficult and dangerous – it can end in death

▓ Brief discussion sessions were held at the end of each day, renamed 'Kickin It', a term used for taking it easy and relaxing with your gang

▓ It was agreed that if the group felt we crossed a line in terms of our assumptions, they would raise a hand (although far too often it was a middle finger instead of a hand) – instead of cursing and swearing – and say 'Salty you' – meaning someone who thinks they know everything. I didn't realise how many assumptions I was making about gang life until I had to listen to this repeated call. Rather than a criticism, it became an observation and was delivered in a humorous not an abusive way

▓ When they worked in smaller groups an appointed note taker would feed back a summary of what the group had discussed to the larger group. We often did this through graffiti. Gangs are infamous for their graffiti skills and use it to express themselves, so they found it easier to represent their discussions through graffiti and then explain if necessary. The person who designs the graffiti is called a 'Tagger' so each group would appoint a tagger to keep notes

Sometimes it's risky to allow the truth of a group's existence to manifest itself within the work. When we used forum theatre to explore alternative behaviours and options in typical gang situations, the interventions were violent and ended in the performance of a death. We could not deny the reality of life for these people on the streets. Equally when financial problems were raised in a forum activity, the interventions suggested were theft and selling drugs. And again, we are not there to judge the right and wrong of the proposed behaviour but to explore it and hopefully gain a better understanding of where it came from. Many projects are commissioned with a view to finding solutions to symptoms, when what is needed is an exploration of causes.

Similarly, the mural the gangs created was a testimony to the journey they took and to the trust and honesty they brought to the telling of that story. However the inescapable reality is that being in a gang is like being in a cult in that it is not easy to leave. Trying to get out can be deadly. Many of the men said afterwards that the sessions had made them more reflective and that they now questioned some of their actions, but that did not mean they would leave the gang. For many the gang is the only family they have and they joined it as young as eleven or twelve years old. Some, however, did go on to use their experiences to work with other young people, telling them about the dangers of being in a gang and the less glamorous side of the lifestyle, and the likelihood of it ending in prison or death.

Principles and practice

- Progression in a workshop requires finding common ground among participants and encouraging sharing
- If observers are to be present, this should only be if it is essential, such as if prison officers are legally required to be there
- Establish clear guidelines with observers about participation and ensure that control of any disruption or outbursts is left to the facilitating team
- Allow groups a ranting phase at the start of the project where they can complain and speak out freely. It is an opportunity to learn a great deal about the group and how to build a trusting relationship with them
- Establish a baseline with each group where activities incorporate things the group enjoy and are familiar with, as this helps place participants in their comfort zone
- Deal openly and non judgementally with the issues involved
- Avoid asking the group to directly give information on the issues involved. It will happen naturally through the activities and then will not feel invasive
- Create a facilitating team, if possible, which has direct knowledge of the issue being dealt with
- Facilitating teams should be mixed in culture, gender and age range where possible
- The facilitating team must not show open disagreement or question one another during the workshop
- Reflection time with the facilitating team can help clear up tensions and deal with questions and uncertainties
- In reflection meetings the team should be encouraged to share their doubts and fears about the project
- Know when and how to acknowledge incidents that might occur, always keeping the interests of the group and the progression of the project foremost
- Research language and terminology and ensure it is appropriate to the group you are working with
- Avoid shrinking away from the reality of participants' lives even if this requires an exploration of issues like violence and abuse

3
Acting up and acting out

After the projects in South America expanded (see Chapter One), various groups approached me asking if I would help set up or run applied theatre projects in their area. These projects dealt with issues such as domestic abuse, alcohol and drug abuse, HIV and AIDS, and work with asylum seekers. I had a full time job and finding the time became a challenge. I turned to people I had trained and worked with over the years and together we decided to create TVO. We were all volunteers, giving up our time to come together and work on projects that inspired us and which, we believed, could make a difference. By 2007 Theatre versus Oppression (TVO) was an official organisation with the goal of using applied theatre to bring about positive change and development through issue based projects around the world. It was a lofty goal, and we weren't quite sure how we would achieve it, or even if we could, but we were all passionate about applied theatre and its potential to bring about change. TVO was awarded UK charity status that year and began to work as a fully-fledged registered charity.

Over the years TVO has run various youth projects, principally for teenagers. This has been with teenagers both in high schools and groups excluded from school due to behavioural issues. School programmes ranged from a one-day workshop to longer projects, tackling issues such as bullying, sex education, integration problems and self-esteem/self-image. Over the years I have worked with children as young as five or six, through to teenagers. Most of the work has been with teenagers considered 'at risk' because their behaviour has involved them with the police.

This chapter is about a youth project which was part of a programme for fourteen to sixteen year olds excluded from school. Most were also experiencing abusive situations at home (drug, alcohol, sexual abuse and often incarcerated parents). The project was sponsored by the centre involved, which received a grant for programme initiatives which exposed young people to various new experiences, generally arts related. The project ran for four months and TVO was commissioned by the local council and an associated theatre.

The programme, called Educational Alternatives was part of a two-year initiative. The students took part in a number of projects over the two years, each project divided into four-month blocks. TVO were allocated the four-month block at the start of the second year. At the end of the two years, depending on their attendance and completion of each project, the students graduated with a qualification, for many the only educational award they would achieve. Some used it to gain entry into a Further Education college where they could complete their high school education. As one group entered the second year, a new group began their first.

Every year, the teenagers were angry at the world, had violent tendencies and significant trust issues – especially, and usually justifiably, with adults. They were far from pleased about doing theatre, especially when told that a performance was part of their project with TVO. They objected on grounds that acting was only for 'queers' and that it affected their street image to be involved in any kind of public performance. TVO's goal, set by the programme organisers, was to use Theatre of the Oppressed methods to study the group's issues from their perspective, and help them gain a better understanding of the world around them. The four months culminated in a devised performance that was used in schools with other troubled teens.

The team consisted of myself and one other facilitator from TVO, plus two or three youth workers who were resident employees with the group. The second facilitator from TVO was usually Luke, who has extensive experience working with 'problem' and 'at risk' youth. My main role was to design the project by working with the needs of each group and helping them create something that would be meaningful to them. It was essential to have someone like Luke in the team, who was accustomed to handling difficult teenagers, had a social work and counselling background and understood where these kids were coming from. Luke himself came from a similar background – an important point of identification for youths who often feel the adults working with them have no real awareness of their lives.

TVO always tries to ensure that at least two facilitators participate in each project. This not only provides a support network, it also enables more perceptive reflection and better development of the work. Being able to bounce ideas off each other and gauge progress based on what is happening in the workshops allows us to build a strong project. Without the benefit of time and space for proper reflection, a luxury few projects can provide until they are over – a lone facilitator can be blindsided by problems that arise or fail to see relevant moments of progress because of over-thinking or over-processing.

While we do not insist on resident workers being present in the workshops, it can be beneficial for the group if handled carefully, so we don't discourage it. Their presence can be integral if the group is difficult and there are risks of violence, especially with today's health and safety rules and extensive legal protocol for working with young people. At the same time, the youth workers need to be sufficiently briefed and open-minded to let us handle situations in our way. It is also an opportunity for the workers to be exposed to our methods and many go on to employ similar methods themselves. Some have even gone on to train with us and take on volunteer positions with TVO.

With Educational Alternatives, I always invited second year graduates of the project to participate with the new group, working as mentors. Apart from a personal sense of achievement which they often gained from this, it gives the group one of their own in an authoritative position, and this is likely to en-gender trust. The young mentors play an essential role as go-betweens while we are building trust between participants and facilitators. Hearing the reflec-tions and opinions of these mentors can help shape the programme to fit the needs of the group and it helps us design projects that work with teenagers' issues of image consciousness. Mentors can also serve as invaluable trans-lators for the street lingo and colloquialisms used.

Through my work with youth groups, gangs and in prisons I have come to accept that we truly do speak different languages. Keeping up with the chang-ing lingo is impossible, especially in different parts of the UK and the USA. I have long since ceased trying to pretend I'm cool enough to understand half the things that are said to me, after landing myself in hot water more than once, so using mentors is a step towards bridging language gaps. Some of these mentors have subsequently trained and become volunteers with TVO.

TVO ran this four-month block with Educational Alternatives over four years. As with so many other excellent youth initiatives, government funding was cut in 2010 and the programme ceased. The groups, generally consisting of twenty fourteen to sixteen year olds, were a challenge from the start. They were labelled 'problem' children by the educational and legal system. They had a background of behavioural problems, exclusion from schools and police records for petty crime, underage drinking and drug offences. Educa-tional Alternatives was not a voluntary project but was set up because of the legal requirement for under-sixteens to be attending some kind of educational programme. The programme was a way of getting young people off the streets and away from drugs and crime.

Each year we worked with the group at the start of their second year on the programme, it was a different group each year, but essentially the same project with the same aims. Yet every project was different. Even when we try to run the same project with a different group it will never be the same because it is the group which shapes it. It can easily change direction, develop differently, produce different reactions and allow for a different sense of engagement. Every year the project took a new and sometimes unexpected direction. Individual understandings of the process differed, as did the contributions and nature of each group's participation. Each project achieved its final goal of a forum style presentation and interaction but the results were different and could not be measured against one another.

Each project concluded with a forum theatre presentation for other young people, tackling topics the group felt affected them most. The groups work-shopped the various issues they faced before choosing their focus area and then we introduced forum and other Theatre of the Oppressed techniques. Each year the issues varied – in the first year the group wanted to look at teenage behavioural issues and the ways in which they lived up to the labels they had been given as bad and disruptive students. In the second year they chose to look at money issues, basically the strategies they employed to get money – which included a number of illegal activities – and the things someone their age needed money for. In the third year we looked at peer pressure and its possible outcomes, and in the final year we looked at teenage pregnancy.

Each topic centred on prominent activities or events in the lives of those particular teenagers at that time. The facilitating team never chose the topic; the ideas always came from the participants. Topics were arrived at through the course of the initial workshops which explored areas that interested, concerned and affected the group. The teenagers had ownership of the project, unlike in the other activities they had been involved with. As the workshops proceeded, it was my job to adapt to their needs and direct our focus onto the areas that most mattered to the group.

The fifteen to twenty teens who made up each group were angry, defensive, negative towards authority of any kind, and generally unwilling to participate. The groups differed in the strength of their feelings and this affected how quickly progress could be made. When TVO came to work with them at the start of their second year inroads had already been made with some of them and cooperation was increasing. With the more difficult groups, the start of the second year was still a battleground. Progress was slow and sometimes difficult to gauge. The problem often lay in the home situation they returned to each day, and this could change the atmosphere in the workshop the next day.

Often a day's planned activities would have to be abandoned to work with new exercises to deal with whatever had occurred at home. The exercises we selected were changeable, designed to acknowledge and help individuals process these events, without them having to talk openly about them. Some of the teenagers would come to the sessions after sleeping in the street the night before because of arguments at home, or wanting to avoid parents who were drunk or high on drugs. Their family situation was generally known to the authorities, but little or no action had been taken. These students would arrive tired, hungry and usually very angry or defensive. The programme organisers were aware of this so provided a basic breakfast for them and, as the group took place in a theatre, they had access to showers. When the workshop began, their focus was often elsewhere and they would look for any opportunity to argue or start a fight. Usually all they needed was space and time to rant about their situation, their anger at their family or the authorities.

Sometimes we would begin by playing a game we call 'Wind Up' in which the students pretend they are clockwork people who have been wound up. The people they would represent were usually the ones they were having problems with. After they were wound up they would begin a rant as that person, repeating the kind of things they would say and how they would normally talk to them. This would continue until the exhausted teenager came to a halt, signifying that they had no more to say. Some would take a break and ask to be wound up again, some would slow down and then suddenly find new life. Each outburst gave them an outlet, often a humorous one, for how they felt they were being treated. It also enabled everyone in the group to find points of identification as they recognised their own situation in another's. At times we would put the immediate topic of the workshop aside to explore the current issue of concern.

Generally I began by dividing them into groups of four or five and then calling out words. They would discuss each word briefly with their group and then make an image to represent it. By watching what images were created I could gauge where unrest lay, or matters that were troubling some of them that day, and I would investigate further by choosing related words. For example, the words family and home, which might seem similar, can reveal a great deal.

The images created often showed violence, drunkenness and division in the family. Home produced images of isolation, fear, even defiance for some. I would then offer words like divorce, alcohol, safety, or words to introduce people such as grandparents, siblings and parents. Although the exercise suggests the words are random, I knew that the students would make a link with the previous images, telling us a story in the process. In the same way, an image of school could reveal a problem there, a result of the problems someone still attending school was facing, or the resentment felt at no longer being a part of the education system which alienated them from their peers.

If one person was particularly outspoken or unable to settle one day because of what had occurred the night before, I would ask him to work in silence, using others to create an image of the problem and an image of its current outcome, without explaining what had actually happened. The group would then try to piece together the story, first in silence and then with dialogue. Once the sketch was underway, the person whose story it was would be instructed that he could shout the command 'Change your intentions!' to the characters at any time, and as often as he chose. This gave the person with the issue a chance to control the direction and the possible outcome of the situation. Gaining control over the sketch acted as a substitute for the real life situation that he felt he had lost control of. The exercise also helped the group see different perspectives, as the intentions changed.

Each year when I began working with a new group, I would ask them to work in groups to complete certain initial activities. The first was to work in smaller groups and come up with three hopes and fears they had for working with us. These were then presented to the larger group, before being written out and pinned up on a wall for the duration of the project. This helped us to gauge the general feelings of the group and their expectations for the work. These lists would be revisited frequently throughout the project to check that the fears were being dealt with and the hopes realised. The group were also given opportunities to revise their hopes and fears as the project developed, our goal being to eventually remove all the fears.

The second task was to complete a set of rules for the workshops. The students again worked in groups to come up with ideas about this. They then presented their ideas to the whole group and the acceptance or rejection of all rules was democratically agreed upon. These rules were also documented and posted on the wall for the duration of the project. The next stage was that the group had to decide what the repercussions would be for breaking these rules. Rules are easier to enforce when created by the groups themselves and they are more willing to accept a 'perceived' punishment when they have decided upon it, rather than seeing it as adult authority – with whom they already have an antagonistic relationship – enforcing its will.

Rules and punishments created are usually very much on teenage terms. Sometimes we will offer guidance and propose ideas but even our ideas must go to the democratic vote. Final rules and repercussions have included the following:

- no use of cell phones during the workshop. Repercussion: phone will be removed by the facilitators until the end of the day
- no fighting in the theatre or within a three-block radius. Repercussion: expelled from the group for that day
- no late arrivals without proper justification. Repercussion: late arrivals must tidy up the workshop room and break rooms at the end of the day
- no unauthorised smoking breaks. Repercussion: the whole group lose a break
- no spitting on each other. Repercussion: the person spitting is not allowed to participate in any of the games for the rest of the day

Often the list of rules was extensive and contained things we considered unnecessary, but they were not our rules to make or criticise. We only used our authority when repercussions were to include violence or some act of aggression. For example, in the first year, one rule was that we had to ensure the workshops were fun and the repercussion was that they were free to key our cars or slash our tyres if they weren't. Needless to say, we ensured that that one did not get past the democratic vote! The point was that they truly felt they had a right to act out in this way. It took much discussion about the nature of repercussions and rules to hone down the proposed list. On another occasion a rule to stop excessive swearing had the repercussion that we were permitted to swear excessively in return. Tempting as this was, we once again discussed and rejected anything that went along these lines. The rules gave the group a sense of responsibility, but it also gave us something to fall back on. If a rule was broken we would point it out and ask them to check what the repercussion was. If they then complained, we reminded them that these were things they had decided and agreed upon, and the complaints and arguments stopped.

The smoking, which was widespread in every group we worked with, proved a major problem as addiction levels were high and the need for breaks intense. I quickly made an agreement with the group allowing regular short smoking breaks on the condition that each week we cut them down. The agreement was also that if they were allowed smoking breaks they, in turn, would promise to smoke only cigarettes. By the end of the project we were usually on a relatively normal break schedule that was respected by everyone. It took us three months to achieve this.

My priority is to try to create an ensemble, a group who can and will work together. Although they have been together for a year by then they are usually extremely divided. They are aggressive and insulting to one another and tend to stay with their own clique of friends. The games tend to present some immediate problems. Smoking and drinking habits have dramatically reduced their fitness levels and physical exercise of any kind is challenging for most of them. Some of them also expressed unwillingness to participate in the games at first. I have found this to be rare except for teenage groups, and when it has occurred is more a reflection of poor planning on my part or choosing inappropriate games.

I don't force anyone to participate but I do make two rules very clear. First, they can sit at the side and watch, but they must not leave the room or talk. Second, they cannot advise the others what to do or shout instructions. I then ensure we play games which will make the observer want to instruct the others and give them advice, so they become frustrated that they are not a part of the activity.

A game such as The Human Knot seldom fails. Participants form a circle, shoulder to shoulder, each placing first one hand in the middle of the circle to grasp another hand, then putting their other hand in the middle, to grasp a different person's hand. Without letting go of the hands they are clasping they must now untangle themselves to create a circle. This simple exercise quickly creates frustration in the observer on the outside, for whom the solution always seems simple.

The game Minimum Surface Contact has a similar effect. Participants use each other's bodies and objects to give themselves the least possible contact with the floor. For example a group of five is told to come together so that they only have a total of three feet and one hand touching the ground. They must quickly work out how they can join together to achieve this. Whenever someone has pulled out, I choose games I know they would find fun and that will induce much laughter. The person sitting on the side then usually feels left out and asks to be a part of what is happening. What is essential is that participating is their decision, while I as facilitator must manipulate what is happening towards achieving the desired result.

The group in the first year looked at behavioural issues and related them to things that had happened to them. They liked the idea that forum gave them a chance to rewrite their stories by showing alternatives that would have reshaped events. We took basic situations such as their issues at home, the behaviour which had led to them being excluded from school, lack of money and ways in which they tried to obtain cash, or peer pressure issues that had them involved in petty crime, drinking or even drugs. In each case we used forum to explore the idea that alternatives existed. Many could not see how their problems could have ended any differently and were curious to explore the fact that other possibilities might exist. The performance they put together featured a teenager who was classified as having ADHD and who was not performing well in school, had problems at home, was being bullied and who, after several warnings, was finally excluded from school for behavioural problems.

The group built each short scene by drawing on their own experience, yet did not make a link between what they saw as the play and any similarities with themselves. Even though they had used their own experiences, they did not see the characters in the play as like themselves. I often find that groups, especially young people, will explore an issue associated with their own situation, yet remove themselves from any identification with it. I think it is important to allow for that removal until they are ready to see it themselves. For example in domestic abuse work, victims are often critical of the victim portrayed in a performance, and abusers insist that it was different for them (see Chapter Five). Identification and acceptance come with time but no one can make that identification for them: it must be allowed to take as long as it needs before they recognise the similarity.

After we had been rehearsing the play for a few weeks, one of the boys stopped in the middle of a scene and said to the others, 'Hey I think this play's about us! We're just like the people in it!' Then he turned to me in shocked realisation, 'Jennifer, I think we might all have ADHD!' The group laughed and started to talk among themselves about all the links, acknowledging that the characters in the play were really them and looking at how they were classified because of their behaviour. The realisation was entertaining, but it was also a turning point for the group as they gained a new awareness about themselves.

When working with a piece of forum theatre, I use exercises from Boal's Theatre of the Oppressed to explore the issue from different angles. In Stop and Think, the participants are asked to stop time and again during a scene and relay what they believe is going through their character's mind at that moment. This gives the players a chance to rationalise how our thoughts do not always match our words, and how we hear what is said to us through the filters of our own judgment. In Stop and Justify, they are again stopped at various points throughout a scene, but this time to justify their character's actions or what they've said. This can help the students to understand their actions better or to realise that their actions cannot be justified as they do not match the situation. This exercise helps teenagers see how they are aggravating a situation without realising it, or even setting out with that intention in mind.

We might use the Softly Softly mode, where participants replay a scene, usually one depicting intense emotion then, at a command, have to speak as quietly as possible and move in slow motion. This makes them observe what is happening around them and forces them to listen intently to what is being said. Another exercise is Agora Mode, where the person with the issue is removed from the scene and the others are asked to discuss the situation in their absence. This too helps people to see that there are different points of view involved in every situation. We also use Angel versus Devil scenarios. While a character speaks a monologue based on the sketch, the angel and devil inside him sit behind him on either side, whispering his thoughts and intentions from their perspective. This helps the students think about how every action has a reaction (details on all these methods can be found in the glossary of games and exercises).

Sometimes the exercises function to improve acting and character building, but all have the potential to aid deeper exploration of the issue. In one exercise, Stop and Think, the players are asked to freeze at different places in the scene and relay what is going on in the character's head just then. This helps them identify their own thoughts and emotions about the issue being portrayed. Similarly in Stop and Justify, they freeze and try to justify their character's actions at a given moment. These exercises are productive because they help improve the performance, but at the same time they are subtly building deeper understanding of behaviour and awareness of different perspectives.

The group particularly enjoyed Boal's exercise, Rashomon, inspired by Japanese filmmaker Akira Kurosawa's study in multiple perspectives. This improvisatory technique highlights the ways our rigid patterns of perception can create a negative view of others and feed our prejudices and even hatred. In Rashomon the protagonist creates an exaggerated image involving his whole body, of how he felt and saw each of the other characters during the preceding scene. These images are referred to as masks. Each actor is given a mask and the characters then repeat the scene wearing this appointed mask. The other characters then have the same opportunity to create a set of images which become the masks each person will wear during successive improvisations.

A boy in one group, Mike, had been thrown out of his home by his mother and was living with his grandmother. For two years he and his mother had not spoken even though they lived a few streets apart. Mike was indignant. He felt that his mother had overreacted and was completely to blame for the situation. As we were practising forum, he asked if we could use the story of his fall-out with his mother. Volunteering a story so early in the process is unusual so it was clear Mike wanted to try to work it through. We prepared and presented a forum scene which depicted the last fight Mike had with his mother, when she threw him out of the house and told him never to come back. In the fight it became clear that there were ongoing problems in the relationship which all surfaced in this final fight. They centred on the fact that Mike had dropped out of school, was hanging with a bad crowd, smoking, not working and had been stealing money from his mother to pay for cigarettes and alcohol. It was also revealed in the sketch that his parents had adopted a young African boy and they believed Mike was setting him a bad example.

Other youths in the group volunteered alternative approaches through the forum exercise. Some suggested ways Mike could have backed down in the argument with his mother so it would not lead to such a dramatic conclusion, such as apologising and agreeing to look for a job. Some suggested that he was jealous of the attention his adopted brother was receiving and that he confront his mother about this. Another was that he break from the crowd he was hanging with and spend more time with his family. Mike remained unmoved throughout, defiant. His mother was in the wrong so none of the compromises or reconciliations were acceptable. Since leaving home Mike had got a job and improved many aspects of his lifestyle, which had, he agreed, been wrong. He was dismissive about being jealous of his adopted brother to whom, he revealed, he was very close and still saw frequently. But he remained outraged that he had been thrown out of the family home and felt this was inexcusable. After each suggestion, Mike felt we were proving how right he was.

We then tried out Stop and Think, and Agora, in search of a different perspective. Mike sat shaking his head at every attempt, unwilling to even contemplate a perspective that differed from his own. It looked as though the only possible way to advance was to look at the different perspectives involved and so I suggested we use Rashomon. I spoke to the group about how our perception shapes the way we see people and often give us a one dimensional view – that, for example, we associate someone who creates a sensation of fear in us with a frightening image of them or that we will see someone we are in love with only through eyes of love. Our feelings are generally more complicated, but in a conflict we tend to narrow our perception of people down to the role they play in our lives. To Mike his mother was evil and unfair, his father sat on the fence not taking sides, his adopted brother was caught in the middle trying to please everyone, and Mike himself felt like the victim, abandoned and unloved. I asked him to associate an exaggerated image of these concepts with each person involved. The idea is to see the image as if it were a mask that can be handed to each of the characters to wear. This mask is only one perspective but the characters will be limited to presenting only this perspective.

Mike created an exaggerated image using his whole body, representing how he saw each of the other characters during the scene, including one of how he saw himself in the situation. His mother's mask was witch-like, her face screwed up and her back stooped, her finger pointing accusingly. His father cast his eyes upwards to avoid connecting with anybody in the scene and held out both hands as if weighing up the situation. The adopted brother had his hands over his ears and his mouth open in a silent scream. Mike himself was bent over in a defeated position, shoulders hunched, head cast down, brow furrowed and teeth gritted as if to say he couldn't understand. The players in turn, took on this image, and 'wore' it like a mask in preparation for repeating the scene.

The restrictions on movement and speech that the masks enforce are revealing. With his eyes cast up, Mike's father could not see anybody else and was oblivious to what was happening around him. The silent scream that shaped the brother's mouth prevented him speaking coherently and being heard. The mother's pointing finger made her aggressive before she even spoke. Her stooped back meant that to talk to Mike she would have to turn her face upwards, yet he had masked himself to be looking down and this meant that as his mother neared him she would be shouting directly into his face. Mike's gritted teeth made him difficult to comprehend and made him come across as aggressive.

80

Each of the other characters then repeats the exercise from their own perspective. Every new mask shows how the scene is viewed by all the people involved, the dialogue and interactions filtered by the masks. The number of improvisations depends on the number of characters. In Mike's scene there were four characters so they had to be replayed four times to show each character's perspective. This exercise offers the opportunity to develop a critical view of people and events. The use of imagery to explore patterns of perception give rise to deformed, incomplete or mistaken impressions. Rashomon challenges notions of stereotypes and promotes greater understanding and empathy.

Keeping their images as masks, the characters then began to improvise the scene once again, repeating the same dialogue and interactions as far as possible within the restrictions of the mask they had been given. A few minutes into the scene, a very upset Mike suddenly asked us all to stop. Sobbing, he told us that the exercise showed his mother as evil, but that this was not the case – she was a good mother with lots of good qualities. He realised that his mask for her represented how he talked about her and thought he saw her, but that it was not a fair representation. Mike asked me to give them a break, then walked off the stage and called his mother, speaking to her for the first time in two years.

Different exercises produce different results, and they affect people in unexpected ways. That is why a project cannot simply be replicated with a new group. To do so would be to ignore what they bring to the table, their unique input as co-collaborators. It is impossible to know what exercise will provide a turning point for the people involved and it is disheartening to see an exercise work well with one group and then have little or no effect on another. It is a constant reminder not to judge the progress of a group by conventional standards, and not to judge oneself as a facilitator by how people react to an exercise. The key lies in the unpicking afterwards, when you have a better feel for what has happened and have had time for reflection. It is through this process that I have taught myself how to adapt exercises, to see how small shifts could produce a different result. This helps me judge things intuitively at the time and be more adept at making changes and creating new exercises on the spot.

Working with teenagers, particularly problematic teenagers, makes for slow progress. Opening sessions are primarily about establishing some form of working relationship and trust that allows us to move forward. This is not easy to achieve. Some individuals have remained closed to the work, aggressive and threatening. With forum work we have run into numerous problems: refusals to allow the audience to interact, abusive responses to audience members who have interacted, or simply a lack of response from the audience. I always try to prepare for such eventualities by, for example, planting people in the audience to start the forum process, but teenagers are unpredictable and no matter how careful the preparation, the outcome has a life of its own.

I have learned to step back from some of the projects when I realise that other members of the team can create a better rapport with the group because of their age and background and that I am not the best person to be leading. In these instances I become the support to the group, not always present but a part of planning and reflection meetings.

Reflections

Working with young people brings its own challenges. They need to be constantly sold on what is happening and they rarely enter the projects with automatic trust for those running them. I would leave a session feeling discouraged because I had achieved so little and the group were getting nowhere. It can be difficult to have a clear view of the advances made because people need their own processing time and that time will be different for each of them. For that reason it is important not to judge this work by conventional standards of success and failure.

I often talk about how an applied theatre project is like going to see a movie and walking out fifteen minutes before the end. You almost know the outcome, you may be able to guess what it might be, but you don't see it the whole way through – the story is unfinished. Applied theatre work never actually ends; it is complete for the facilitator at a certain stage, but the work continues through the influence on the individual or community in various ways. A successful applied theatre project will leave participants with the skills to integrate aspects of the work in a way that speaks to them as they proceed.

The terms success or failure are too simplistic to be applied to projects that require assessment by criteria such as reflection and awareness. Some days a project can flow, other days you can leave feeling battered and bruised, wondering what is blocking progress. Some days the participants will be open and keen, other days less so. None of it is personal and it is usually related to the issues being worked on. I have had days when I've gone home promising myself that this will be the last project I do. Interestingly, this feeling usually comes directly before a breakthrough with that group and this reminds me why I am doing what I am doing, why it will not be the last project I do.

Sometimes groups are formed to create a project in applied theatre, but at other times the applied theatre project is one slot in an ongoing programme. Often these projects end on a high – there is a performance, great participation and feedback, and the group feel they have made real progress. But then the facilitating team leave and it is all too easy for a group to lapse back to how they were before. I have learned how important follow up work is for each group, not only to check on progress and how they might be applying what they have learned from the project, but also because the group will continue processing long after the project has ended. Finding the time to talk with them and explore where they are at after the project is over can be rewarding for the group, but it certainly provides important feedback for the facilitators. Being able to do follow up work depends on factors such as timing, location, and access. So having the permanent workers take part in the project becomes a form of training for them. They see what has been achieved and the process involved and I always spend time with them explaining how they can implement follow up work after we've left.

What I do think is essential is that the last contact with a group is not a performance. There should be at least one meeting afterwards for reflection and discussion. Young people especially will be on a high after a successful performance and they need guiding into the stage that follows, or they will feel a sense of loss and abandonment. We usually organise a follow up workshop to reflect on the project and the outcome of the performance and make a final visit, which is mostly a social occasion. Many of these young people are used to feeling abandoned and have little trust in adults and their ability to be around for them. A social visit shows a continued interest in who they are and what they are doing and is key to the continued building of trust that was set in motion when the project first began.

Principles and practice
- Try to ensure that at two or more facilitators participate in each project to provide a support network and enable more perceptive reflection
- Resident workers being present in the workshops can be beneficial for the group especially if there is for example, a danger of violence
- Resident workers must be sufficiently briefed about the nature of applied theatre work and be open to the process
- It can be productive to create mentors from among the participants from a previous group to help a new one that is dealing with the same issues

- Make rules with the group and, especially with younger groups, decide together what the repercussions of breaking those rules will be
- Running the same project with different groups will always produce different results because it is the participants who shape it
- External events can affect the lives of participants and these should never be ignored in the workshop
- Avoid forcing anyone to take part but do make rules about non-participation
- Avoid making realisations for people, let them make their own as and when they are ready to
- Avoid judging the progress of a group by conventional standards. Traditional concepts of success and failure cannot be used with applied theatre
- Avoid taking things personally or judging yourself as a facilitator by how people react to an exercise. Come back to the unpicking afterwards in reflection meetings when you will have a better feel for what has happened
- Follow up work after the project is complete, where possible. This is an important way to check on progress, as the group will continue processing long after the project has ended. It also provides important feedback for the facilitators
- Encourage the hosting organisation to give some form of in-house after care

4

An alternative approach
to domestic abuse

The houselights dim and the play begins. The stage is stripped bare except for two chairs, a table and a bottle of vodka.

The play is a deceptively simple two-hander about a married couple and the conflict in their relationship that erupts into domestic abuse. Although it is based on the real life experiences of people I came into contact with, I edited the play substantially during its developmental phase, as audiences said they found it unbelievable. This shocked me and I remember sitting in the theatre suppressing the urge to defend its authenticity as a true story. I had to remind myself that there are limits to how much human tragedy we can absorb in the guise of entertainment. The remarkable story had caught my interest because of all that happened, but that did not mean I had to force my audience to swallow it whole. Nor did they need to do so for the play to maintain its impact.

My intention was to present the facts of the story without apportioning blame. In all TVO's work we try to show both sides of an issue in an attempt to understand human behaviour. The audience are often left feeling complicit, as they realise that no situation is as black and white as it may at first appear: the behaviour can be condemned but the reasons behind the behaviour beg to be understood if a way forward is to be found. In the play's development phase an outraged audience member stood up during the post-show discussion to express her disgust with me as writer for 'making' her like the character of the husband. Her fury was in no way abated by my attempts to explain that I had simply told a story, not 'made' her like anyone.

The actors have been instructed to regularly address the audience directly, ensuring they made eye contact with them. The goal is to make the audience complicit in the events of the play because of their reactions, or lack of them. It is not intended to be a comfortable viewing experience for the spectators. Each night I stood at the back of the theatre and watched the reactions around me.

Many would cast their eyes to the floor the moment they thought one of the actors was about to make eye contact with them. Some held the contact as an act of defiance against the abuser, or to express sympathy for the victim. I remember one man sitting in the front row repeatedly opening his programme and pretending he was reading it, using it as a barrier between himself and the stage. Another time I sat behind a couple and watched as the husband became more and more agitated. Finally he lent over to his wife and said, 'Oh God did you bring me here to try to tell me something? Is that me up there?' He later explained that although he was not abusive, he had grown up with a father who was, and his fear was that he was just like him but couldn't see it. At times audience members utter responses to the questions asked them by the actors, some wanting to justify their own reactions or their guilt at liking the abuser. The actors had been strictly instructed to ignore this and not engage with the audience's reactions during the play.

Every performance is followed by a talk-back where the audience, more often than not, talk about their own reactions and feelings, rather than asking questions of the cast or crew. The talk-back became their opportunity to share, offload, explain or justify. Many said that they had had a dilemma, wanting to get up and leave yet finding themselves spellbound, unable to move as they watched the events unravel. Many audience members were victims of abuse, or the family and friends of victims, or social workers, support workers and prison education officers. They spoke about the reality of the play, the language, but also the sensitivity. We never see the wife being beaten and the play balances moments of tenderness with the abuse.

On this particular evening, I sat at the back of the theatre as usual studying the reactions of the public. On occasions the husband, Paul, turns to the audience. He says that they too would have been pushed to such behaviour by the actions and words of his wife and looks to them for agreement; he insists that he was left with no choice, asking some audience member 'you know what I mean?'.

I noticed a middle-aged couple seated a few rows down. The actor playing Paul had targeted the husband with his questions a few times. The husband was clearly engrossed, sitting forward and almost meeting the actor's gaze. His wife kept looking from the actor to her husband. Once Paul makes eye contact with the husband in the audience, 'You know what these women are like', and the husband smiled, nodding slightly in agreement. His wife moves back casting a disapproving and warning glance at her husband. A few minutes later Paul tells the audience, 'She'd push and push and just left me with no damn choice. You know what I mean?' Before the actor could even look at the husband, the wife had turned to him glaring, defying him to dare nod.

Paul continued, once again making direct eye contact with the husband, 'You know, someone just pushes your damn buttons and in your head you imagine slapping them. We all do it, imagine it like. You know what I mean?' The poor husband was sitting nodding in agreement with the actor almost subconsciously, when he suddenly got a slap from his wife, 'Oh, you know what he means do you? Just wait 'til we get home!' As she rebuked her husband for empathising with the abuser, she appeared oblivious to the fact that she had herself become an abuser.

Background

This chapter is about the domestic abuse project TVO began in 2010 and is still working with. I have worked on various domestic abuse situations over the last decade but they have been short term or one-off workshops. The more workshops I carried out, the more I realised how widespread the problem was. I began looking into developing a longer term approach to domestic abuse with TVO based on our applied theatre techniques because we believed there was a demand for a project that would address both the victims and the perpetrators, one that would look at the causes behind abuse. Wherever we set up projects, on whatever topic, the issue of domestic abuse constantly arose in one form or another. It is a problem that knows neither geographical nor cultural boundaries. Whether it was the UK, USA or Africa, we saw the same domestic abuse patterns time and again, the same actions and reactions, the same excuses and reasoning from both sides.

The goal of the project is to work with behavioural patterns as a vehicle towards understanding perspectives and gaining new understandings of the self and in relation to others. Thus we are attempting to work with causes rather than symptoms of abuse. We developed a set of pilot activities for trial workshops in both the UK and USA that would address the needs of the perpetrators and victims separately. These pilot workshops proved successful, attracting enthusiastic reactions from support groups, safety units and prisons and various grant awards to expand the project.

In each location the project began with a play based on the real life experiences of people involved in domestic abuse, called *'Til death do us part*. The play was written following interviews and workshops with perpetrators and survivors of domestic abuse and is based on the story of a married couple, Kerry and Paul. I came to know Kerry through interviews carried out with victims of domestic abuse. Her story was representative of many women I worked with, but some startling factors heightened the problem and attracted me to work on her story for the play. I did not want to do a straightforward story of victim and abuser. Kerry's story clearly showed how she had regularly manipulated Paul through her victim role. I wanted people to understand the complexities in the relationship, the reasons she had stayed with him for so long, the manipulation and control that were going on on both sides. Only then, I believed, could an audience be successfully persuaded to resist a black and white interpretation of the situation.

While Kerry's lines were almost all her own words, as taken from the interviews, Paul's had been sourced from a workshop with a group of men in a support group which provided counselling and therapy for abusive behaviour. Working with these men I was struck by the similarities in their comments and explanations and I realised that Paul could be any one of them. With their assistance and my knowing the true story, I was able to bring Paul's character to life for the play.

The play develops the relationship between the couple mainly through a series of monologues, showing the attraction and love they felt for each other as well as the violence which finally destroyed them. Two main incidents had drawn me to the real life story of Kerry and Paul. The first was Kerry's desperation to stop her alcoholic husband drinking. In her desperation she had made a deal with him: if he stopped drinking, she would also give up something. At Paul's suggestion, and with horrific consequences, she agreed to give up her medication for diabetes. The second factor was Paul's suicide, which he carried out as an act of ultimate dominance over his wife.

The play was developed in stages in front of an audience. The audience provided feedback at each stage and had an opportunity to offer ideas on how the story would develop, and to take part in activities devised from the play itself to explore Kerry and Paul's relationship. It was they who identified key points at which a change in what was said or a different action could possibly alter the outcome. We would return to these moments and play them out with an alternative suggestion offered by the audience and then see if it led to change, or simply a postponing of the previous outcome.

In other activities audience members along with the actors played the members of a support group and discussed the events and behaviour with a counsellor. We also set up a scenario of individual counselling sessions with both Kerry and Paul, where audience members volunteered to take on the role of the counsellor. Many thought this would be easy, but were challenged by the actor remaining steadfastly in character and his consequent lack of cooperation. Audience members discussed how easy many of the exercises appeared in theory, but how when they tried to use them to bring about change, they realised how difficult this must be to actually achieve in real life.

This chapter describes four domestic abuse projects: two working with male convicts in prisons, one in the UK and one in the USA, and two working with female victims in safety unit groups in the UK. TVO has an established UK-based team for these projects, made up of the two actors who perform the play and participate in the follow up exercises, and three facilitators including myself. In the US I helped initiate the project and consulted on it alongside a US based group working in applied theatre. The actors were brought in for the play but both had previous experience of performing in a prison setting. Below I discuss certain aspects of the four projects and the approach and methodology applied in each.

Getting off on the right foot in an American prison

A group of men sit around the closely guarded space waiting for the performance to begin. The men in front of me, aged between twenty-two and sixty, are all in prison for offences relating to physical abuse, from repeated battery to voluntary manslaughter.

Working on projects abroad means I am not always with my own team but work with one already based in the location and which will continue the work I set up. Generally this is not a problem, but in applied theatre things seldom go to plan, and the team need to be able to adapt quickly and instinctively. Familiarity with the people you work with helps. My American team of two facilitators and two actors are accustomed to working with difficult groups and some have experience of working in a prison setting. Using theatre in this way is, however, new to them and I can sense their apprehension as we make our way through the numerous gates and checks to reach the allocated workshop area. None of us speaks, but then the stark conditions and humourless guards do not encourage conversation. I am severely scolded by a surly guard for playing with the drug-sniffing dog that pounces on me, much to the concern of my fellow facilitators. Once it has been confirmed that I am not carrying drugs, we are ushered through the next set of stringent checks.

We have been given a large space to work in, bare but for the vandalised metal benches. Entrances and exits to the area are barred and patrolled by armed guards. Above us is a barred balcony area, also patrolled. It reminds me of certain TV shows and I am both surprised and disturbed by their accuracy. Looking around the space I can't help but notice how different prisons are in American and in the UK. Someone once told me that British prisons are designed for rehabilitation while American ones are intended for punishment. I'm not sure the repeat offender statistics in the UK would bear this out, but the general atmosphere and the attitude of the prisoners is undeniably different. Over the last decade I have conducted workshops in prisons in Central and South America, Africa, the USA and the UK. Each has been a unique and often harsh learning experience.

In the British system prisons are categorised as either 'open' or 'closed' and graded from A to D, with A for prisoners who present the greatest threat to the public and D for the least. Prisoners in category D institutions are granted greater freedom and opportunity for social interaction. In South and Central America the prison system is plagued by issues such as overcrowding, poor sanitary conditions, drugs trafficking, gang wars and poorly trained staff. In Africa added considerations have to be given to any proposed project due to levels of corruption within the prison system and epidemic problems of AIDS/HIV. In the US, the country with the highest documented incarceration rate in the world, there is a heavier armed presence due to overcrowding and gang problems. Rehabilitation programmes take a back seat.

My accent greatly entertains the men. They make analogies with the characters in Danny Boyle's infamous movie from the 90s, *Trainspotting*, about Scottish drug culture. Sarcastically they request a translator, and query whether or not I come with my own subtitles. When I slow down and enunciate my words with extra care, I am accused of mocking them and treating them like idiots, although their wording is rather more explicit and colourful. At first I am taken aback that they find me difficult to understand, as I have conducted countless workshops in the USA without problems and my accent, in my opinion, is mild. As we progress it becomes clear that they are trying to get a reaction out of me and I need to remember that before they succeed.

I am used to Americans telling me how 'quaint' my accent is, not to mention the occasional lost in translation moment. While that can be irritating, it has never before felt threatening. Looking out at thirty disgruntled men, sitting spread-eagled in a macho territorial display, is a different matter. One man, a gang leader, is particularly uncooperative. Every time he catches my eye, and a little too often even when he doesn't, he lifts his hand as if it is a gun, takes aim and shoots at me. The last thing I want to do is show them my discomfort or annoyance, a bad start to any workshop. Unnerved as I am by this play of shooting, I have been threatened enough by real guns not to be fazed by an imaginary one. I joke back about my accent, the fact that we are two nations divided by the same language and apologise if I am difficult to understand. Immediately many seek to reassure me there is no problem and I needn't worry, genuinely concerned that I might feel offended. They kindly suggest that my fellow facilitators, the Americans, can translate for me if there are any difficulties. Suppressing my irritation at this unintentional insult, I move on with the workshop.

We begin with a short discussion to lay down some ground rules for watching the play extracts – rules about interrupting, respecting the actors and the space. I explain the 'time out' concept we use when working with issue based projects or when presenting plays that could cause an extreme reaction in the audience. If the material becomes overwhelming for the viewer, or if they feel discomfort, they can signal that they need a time out. At this signal, we stop what we are doing for a couple of minutes. Sometimes we play a game to divert attention from the subject matter; most often the group just need time to exhale before continuing or have a quick chat about what they are feeling. The men, like most groups, dismiss the need for a time out, insisting they will have no problems. My experience has shown that they will need and use this at some point during the workshops, though usually not at the beginning. The time out is the same concept a sports coach might use to check in with his players and go over the game plan. Over time, as trust develops, the parti-cipants tend to relax and warm to the idea, instead of seeing it as a display of weakness.

I chat with the men about their concept of theatre and a few share their ex-periences. Most mention a play they took part in at school, or watched their children perform. None have been impressed by these experiences and they become extremely vocal in their opinion that all actors are 'gay', citing musicals as proof. The two American actors catch my eye and I sense their uncertainty. After some discussion, I tell them that the play they are about to see is nothing like what they have described. I explain that it will probably make them uncomfortable and that I need them to always remember that this is theatre; while the story is real, it will be performed by actors, not the people whom the story is about. They scoff at my concern, but this is an important point. I have often found with issue-based groups that they cannot separate the actor from the character, the fiction from fact.

The men are growing restless, their curiosity about the play piqued. They are keen to move on. The actors enter the bare stage area to a hushed room. We have no scenery; all our applied theatre plays are intended to be easily trans-portable and to focus entirely on the issue. *'Til death do us part* requires two chairs and a small table with a bottle of vodka on it. For our performance we have the chairs and table, itself a challenge to the prison authority's wishes that they be screwed down, In the end we compromise, the table and one chair are screwed to the ground and one chair is left free for us to move around. The vodka bottle has been replaced with a plastic water bottle to comply with prison regulations. I have removed the label and replaced it with a rapidly written one that simply says 'vodka'. At the request of the prison officers, who are concerned lest someone try to steal the water bottle in the hope that it does contain alcohol, I tell the men that it only contains water.

As the actors begin, I note that the men are a more vocal audience than I am accustomed to. I have carefully selected key extracts as time is limited and I fear the whole play would eat up too much time, and be too much for the men to sit through as a first experience of this kind of theatre. The extracts focus on moments leading up to violent outbursts by both husband and wife. Grunts and other approving or disapproving noises emanate from the prisoners as the story begins. They exchange looks with one another and, to my discom-fort, laugh at inappropriate moments. Some sit immobile, looking straight ahead at a point beyond the actors in an attempt to disassociate themselves from the whole experience.

As we advance through the extracts, the intensity increases and we come closer to scenes where the husband will turn violently on the wife. This is im-plied but never shown. The play then jumps to the husband or wife address-ing the audience about what happened. The husband usually rationalises his behaviour, seeking out and usually gaining a sympathetic response from the spectators. Each time we come closer to a scene where it appears the hus-band will beat his wife, the men become more animated and restless.

And then it happens, the first time the husband advances to beat his wife. Im-mediately the men jump to their feet clapping and cheering, high-fiving one another amid shouts of support to the husband. The actors turn to me stunned, uncertain how to proceed. I look on in horror, sick to my stomach, wondering what I had been thinking to show the play here.

I sit watching the men openly display their enthusiasm and hunger for vio-lence, and try to dismiss my fears. I have to remind myself, not for the first time, to trust the methods we use. A group's reactions can temporarily knock you off balance, or make you question your choices, even yourself, but ulti-mately you must trust the work. I know the men's reactions to the play are defence mechanisms kicking in as a reaction to the fear of being judged and their desire to justify themselves. I know sometimes I just have to let things take their course rather than reacting to them or trying to stop them. If I try to stop a reaction while it is happening, what follows will be about my actions rather than about the reactions of the group.

As the play continues, the noise dies down and the enthusiasm for violence slowly dies with it. Despite this, I know the planned activities need to be changed right away, to deal with these demonstrations of support for abuse, otherwise the workshops that follow will be flawed. While things that happen during a project may not always be openly addressed, we must ensure they are woven into the activities. Failure to do so can be interpreted as support; just as addressing it head on will be viewed as rebuke and evoke feelings of being judged, and this will impede progress.

I decide to move on with a variation of Boal's forum theatre, avoiding the planned discussion and activity that centred on creating a background for each character. I take the scenes that caused the strongest and most vocal re-actions of support and tell the group we will replay them. The difference will be that this time they are to shout 'STOP' at any point they feel the husband could choose a different course of action. The husband is not the traditional oppressor in any of the selected scenes, something forum would normally call for. However I feel this gives the men a chance to think of and present alternatives to the actions they have not only supported but exercised in their own lives. For me to stand in front of them and suggest alternatives is futile – they have to discover them themselves.

Doing forum with problem groups, particularly in prisons and with gangs, means you frequently get suggestions that are more violent and criminal in nature that what has been shown or implied by the play. It is important not to reject these, as they relate to the lives of these people. Discovering alternative behaviours requires an exploration and understanding of the normal be-haviour and reactions of the participants when they have found themselves in these situations. In this version of forum the men will still come up and re-place the husband, acting out their suggestions rather than explaining them from the safety of an audience position. The men in prison settings often come to enjoy forum immensely. Many have problems articulating what they want to say in a discussion, but in forum they gain confidence and enjoy the theatrical element. There are rules to follow, such as no physical contact, and as the principal facilitator (Boal's Joker) I have to be ready to step in quickly to end a scene, move things on, or help promote a discussion from the audience about the possible outcomes or pros and cons of suggestions put forward.

Over the next forty minutes men replace the husband and suggest a variety of ideas for alternative action. As expected, the first suggestions are of more abusive approaches and cause more laughter. One of the first ideas presented: beating the wife earlier on to prevent her becoming so annoying, receives great support from the men. We progress to ideas of locking the wife in a room, threatening her violently at the outset, insulting her into submission and threatening to leave her, or to beat the children. After each suggestion is acted out, the men are asked how it might change the outcome. They soon acknowledge that nothing is changing and that the situation often becomes worse.

Now the group move to a different tack. New suggestions are made: the husband might walk out and go to the pub to avoid confrontation, or turn the volume up on the TV to drown her out, or try to reason with her about why things are escalating, or use counting or similar techniques as a way to control his temper when he feels he will explode. Although these suggestions offer some improvement, they are all temporary fixes and the men quickly acknowledge this. This helps us arrive at the first step: the men recognise that sticking a band-aid on the problem is temporary and addresses only symptoms not causes. The abuse is a symptom; we need to look at causes if we are to effect any behavioural change. This may seem obvious, we could stand in front of the group and state it, but we would achieve nothing. These exercises help the men make the realisations for themselves. The realisations are significant. They take them by surprise, opening them to the possibility of developing the work further.

The men discuss how replacing the husband was leading nowhere and suggest that they replace the wife instead. This is the second step: they are suggesting a new move which will enable them to look at the issue from a perspective other than their own. I am wary about asking a group in a prison setting to take on an opposite sex role as it can lead to mockery and, if done too soon, can come across as degrading the victim. The men however are the ones who suggest it, when they are frustrated with the husband and trying to find a way forward in the situation.

As they play the wife, the men offer sensible and logical solutions, yet feel frustrated that the actor playing the husband reacts abusively almost every time. The actor's behaviour is in keeping with his character and in the accompanying discussions the men acknowledge that they would do the same, although they insist it was 'unfair' on the wife as she has 'no hope of doing or saying the right thing'. They remark how their own ideas would aggravate the situation and would infuriate them if they were the husband. One member of the group declares: 'It doesn't matter what she does, if I've got it in my head that I'm going to hit her, I will. She doesn't have a chance because it's got nothing to do with her why I feel that way.' The other men nod in agreement. That breakthrough enables the workshops to begin.

The play and exercises that followed allowed us to open up the topic of domestic abuse without saying directly that we were doing so. The men made admissions freely and had begun to reflect on their own actions. To get to that point, it had been necessary to grant them a space in which they could laugh, act out and trial ideas that had perpetuated further abuse. We were now in a position to start working on exercises that look at behaviour patterns and what causes them, exercises such as Significant Ages. The men would go on to make their own observations and decide whether or not they wanted to change their behaviour.

A tentative step towards rehabilitation

The twenty-four men were brought to the workshop room from different areas of the prison. As they entered they nodded to one another before taking their seats in the circle of chairs. We watched how they chose their seats, who they opted to sit next to, who chatted to friends, and who remained silent. When just over half of the group had arrived Ian was brought in. In his early thirties, with a slightly threatening air of authority, Ian was tall, good looking and smartly dressed (as a private class D prison, the men were allowed to wear their own clothes). He nodded towards the chair he wanted, one that had already been taken, and the men immediately scattered, leaving not only that chair free but also those on either side. As the remaining men entered, they avoided the seats on either side of Ian, bringing extra chairs into the circle to avoid invading his space. They all greeted him and he returned the greeting amicably. It was clear that Ian was top dog. At the back of the room was tea, coffee and water and the men were free to help themselves. The room looked like a normal workshop room in any college or school. The windows were locked but not barred. The prison guards and education officers, curious but open to the work, kept in the background, and this supported the non-threatening atmosphere.

We moved to sit with the men in the circle and I took one of the seats next to Ian, causing an exchange of glances and raising of eyebrows. It was important to build the idea that everyone in the room was equal for this work, not just for the relationship between the participants and facilitators, but also among the participants themselves. The others in my team sat scattered in the available chairs to avoid creating a 'them and us' situation.

We began with an activity before any discussion about the project. Pieces of paper had been placed around the room, each with a different word on it. The words were all related to imprisonment and abuse, although some had only a tenuous connection. They included: judge, jury, cell, family, discipline, police, weekend, rehabilitation, uniform. The men were invited to gather at one of the papers and discuss the associations and understandings they had of the word with whoever else was standing there. After one minute the participants would be instructed to move to another piece of paper and repeat.

The tight time limit was designed to avoid awkward silences and to give the impression that we were racing against time to encourage them to speak out. They could revisit a word if they felt they had more to say about it. Members of the facilitating team were on standby to jump in, to prevent only one person standing at any of the words, but this proved unnecessary. As I had suspected, the men moved quickly to the people they were most comfortable with rather than being drawn to a particular word. The exercise allowed me to observe the cliques in the group, who the outsiders were, who the leaders were and who would be the most vocal and opinionated.

As in the US prison, we said a little about the play they were about to watch, 'Til death do us part, and I explained the time out procedure they could use if they became too uncomfortable, while making it clear that some discomfort was to be expected. As this was a category D prison it was more relaxed than the US prison, the men were more accustomed to the concept of working together on prescribed activities. The prisoners sat in a semi-circle around a cleared area that would serve as a stage – there was a distance of no more than 2 to 2.5 metres between the two actors and the first row of spectators.

Before starting the play, I introduced my team and myself and thanked the prisoners for agreeing to participate in the workshops – a sign up activity for which they could receive points for good behaviour. Considering their other choices such as weight lifting, a DIY class and literacy support, this was not a light option for any of them. I mentioned that I had recently done a similar project in a prison in the US and I shared the problems the inmates had with my accent. The men promptly became protective, insisting that there was nothing wrong with my accent. The common enemy across the ocean, albeit a rather unexpected and unintended one, established a basic sense of trust and unity. We all understood one another.

We began the performance of the play. I moved to the back of the room. The prison guards, who had been briefed beforehand, spread out around the sides and rear of the room, sitting unobtrusively as members of the audience. The idea was to be ready to move in and call a 'time out' ourselves if we saw any potential trouble. Our job is not to watch the play but to observe the audience. In the same way as the games we use, the play is vital to understanding the emotions, reactions and needs of the group.

At first there was some chuckling and turning around to exchange looks. The men quickly understood what the play was going to be about and many sat back and folded their arms defensively. Ian, the top-dog, had insisted on having a front row seat, where he remained immobile and emotionless throughout. Only when the play was over did he react, leaning forward, his head cradled in his hands for a few minutes. The reactions of the other men varied. Some laughed uncomfortably in certain scenes, looking around for support from the others. Some began to mutter comments about what was happening such as 'You know he's going to hit her now', 'Oh no, you know what's coming', 'It's the drink'. Most shifted around uncomfortably on their seats.

Afterwards I asked the men what they had thought about the play. One of the most articulate of the group spoke up: 'Are you asking for a critical response 'cos if you are, it was really good but far too long. We're not in a theatre and these are not comfortable seats!' The play is seventy minutes long. We all laughed and the men took this as a cue to speak freely about the play. They were overwhelmingly critical of both the husband and wife, but said the hardest part to watch was when the husband had spoken to his child. The child is never seen but is addressed as if he is standing offstage. During the scene all the men had turned towards where the child was supposedly standing and become acutely agitated. One explained that he had sat on his hands to stop himself from getting up and punching the husband for talking to the child as he did. The others agreed. This allowed for development at a later stage in the workshop about the involvement of children in abusive home situations. It also lead to discussion about what the men had been through and witnessed when they were children.

After the discussion, the men's first task was to build the life and background of each character from the play. The group found this easy and fun to do. We began by sitting in a group and asking them to discuss the couple's possible family background and education, their first job, and how they had met. The men became so engrossed in creating this background that we no longer needed to ask them questions. They debated their opinions among themselves and rationalised their conclusions. They began drawing on their own lives to create the background of the characters. Some groups picked up on subtle inferences and lines from the play that other groups did not and supported all their conclusions with evidence directly from the play. What fascinated me most was their ability to quote lines from the play extensively and accurately. This showed the attention they had paid to the play, but also emphasised its accuracy, as the men recognised lines they too would use.

This exercise was built on through simple creative exercises done in a few workshops. For example, they wrote birthday cards to and from the husband and wife and discussed how to word birthday cards to the children, deciding unanimously that only the wife would be involved in that. They planned a typical weekend, their favourite food, a supermarket list and favourite songs, even a school parent night. The delight of prisoners in being able to plan a simple excursion like a trip to the supermarket is hard to imagine. All these activities required an understanding of the characters, but also of themselves. As the men rationalised their choices for every new creative exercise, they showed deeper understanding of themselves and their situations without realising that they were doing so.

I then asked a disarmingly simple question for the men to discuss. Did the husband and wife love one another? The question opened the proverbial can of worms, as for the first time the men became divided in their opinions. Most insisted that they did not. They talked about the wife having low self-esteem and the husband having a drink problem which, in their opinion, meant they were not in a position to understand what love meant. However the real division came with deciding whether or not the couple had ever loved one another. The men began citing examples from their own lives. A smaller group became very defensive about their conviction that the couple did love one another and that that was why they had stayed together. This outraged some of the men, who insisted that a woman who stays with a man who beats her after children come along is a bad mother who does not understand the meaning of love. Their arguments were fascinating and revealed much about their way of seeing the world.

I then introduced the group to image theatre. I asked them to make groups and explained that in turn, one person from each group would mould the others to create an image that represented the story or issue of the play. They created images of the couple in the midst of an abuse scene with a child hiding in the background, watching intently; of the husband and wife facing one another, each with their hands held up in frustration; of the wife looking as though she was complaining to the husband while he stood with his back to her, fists clenched; and of scenes of various counselling type sessions, each of which made evident a lack of cooperation or progression.

After this they discussed ways in which the images had differed or been similar. During group discussions I avoid sitting with any group or standing anywhere that gives the impression I am listening in. If I participate in these discussions it can quickly turn into a teacher centred activity, where they look to me for guidance and approval. I want the group to have the freedom to discuss openly, without fear of saying the wrong thing, or feeling they have to say the right thing. It also enables me to observe the group again, noting participation and comfort levels and spotting anyone who seems to be on the outside, unwilling or unable to participate, as it is my responsibility to design activities to ensure inclusion.

With small group discussions I always give the group less time than they need, so that the discussions are normally ended mid-flow. If a discussion has begun to dry up, uncomfortable silences can set in, or the subject can be changed and participants wander off topic. Ending a discussion mid-flow leaves the group still engaged and keen to continue. After the individual group discussions we reconvene as a whole and I ask if they want to share anything about the discussions. This feedback, while brief, allows for sharing and development and helps me gauge how the group as a unit is progressing.

After they had created their images I asked the men to return to their groups and this time create an image from their own lives that the play had made them think about. This exercise is also conducted in silence but this time they are to insert themselves into the image once it is complete. This is a demanding exercise and it is important not to underestimate how emotionally, mentally and physically draining this kind of work can be for people, especially when the concepts are new to them. In a later workshop I return to these images to build on them, but I ensure that advances are made in small steps so the process is not overwhelming.

What was striking about the images – and surfaced in the discussion that followed – was how many men portrayed scenes from their own childhood. Many commented that they had never before made a link between what they saw and experienced as children and their actions as adults. Only after they created their images did it occur to them that they were repeating patterns. To an outsider such a link may seem obvious, but identifying patterns in our own and others' behaviour is more complicated when we are inside the issue. These exercises enabled them to take a step back and look at situations from different angles and perspectives and this opened up new understandings.

For the next development I introduced Boal's forum theatre, using various scenes from the play to look at possible alternative outcomes. In traditional practices of forum theatre the oppressed character, the protagonist, is the initial focus, with spectators replacing the protagonist and showing what they might do in that situation. This can later be extended to replace the antagonist or any other character in the scene. The group must attempt to alter the course of the dramatic action by offering alternative solutions. In this instance I told the men they could replace the husband or the wife.

The group agreed on three scenes to apply the forum process to. At first the men chose to replace the wife, but as they progressed they opted increasingly for the husband. After each intervention we briefly discussed what had happened, the outcomes and possible consequences. In the beginning they mostly felt the wife was aggravating the situation so they made her appease her husband. Each discussion however came back to the notion that this was simply postponing the inevitable, as the husband would look for excuses to turn on her. So the men started making the wife more affirmative, having her walk away from an escalating argument, or even leave the husband. The men were quick to see how this could provoke greater violence and did not solve the issue in the long term. Now the men began replacing the husband and looking for ways to change his behavioural pattern.

One of my jobs in applied theatre is to acknowledge that everyone has a story to tell – to acknowledge that everyone has a voice to be heard. By giving every-one a voice, a platform from which to speak, and an audience with which to engage, stories are often released. The men engaged in activities that allowed them to explore the topic of conflict, such as Boal's Fighting Cocks where they work in pairs, one accusing the other of having done something wrong. The other person has to defend and justify his actions. I make it a rule that the action the person is being accused of is not stated, so we do not know what caused it. This helps to show the cyclical nature of arguments, and how, when an argument begins, it rapidly becomes about other things and the original issue is forgotten. At all times the men made the decisions about the direction the work took. They later told me that what had engaged them most was the fact that they were at last being listened to, and their realisation that much of their anger and frustration stemmed from feeling they were not being heard.

One of our last activities with this group is one I named The Bigger Story. The group forms a large circle and the actors from the play join as their characters. Everyone in the circle takes on a role associated with the characters – a son, daughter, grandfather, employer and so on. Every group chooses different characters based on their own perceptions of the situation and the people they view as central to the story. When I did the same activity with a women's group the characters involved caseworkers, other women in the safety unit, friends and family. The men added new roles: cellmate, judge, police officer, lawyer, prison guard and mate from the pub and volunteered for these roles. When a female role came up I gave the men the option to change it to a male role. When working in prisons, men playing female roles risk being mocked about it afterwards by the other inmates. The men said defiantly that they had no problem playing a female role and declared their support for one another.

Once the characters have been selected, two are chosen to go into the middle of the circle and strike up a conversation. After a couple of minutes, one is removed and a new person enters. This often means that characters who would not normally cross paths will suddenly find themselves in the centre, forced to conduct a conversation with an unlikely counterpart. Each time a new conversation begins the circle must respect the information revealed and can build on it.

Certain basic rules apply. Only the facilitator can change who is in the centre. No physical contact is permitted. The two in the centre must remain there for the time allocated even if they choose not to speak. There can be no leaving the circle unless a time out has been requested, in which case the individual will step out and one of the team will stay with them until they are ready to return. This exercise is always entertaining and at the same time revealing. The participants are not put off by the theatricality and they immerse themselves in the developing story, eager to see what will happen next, as if they were following a soap opera. At times the story will take a new direction, a new main character might develop, or a new issue that underlies the one we originally began dealing with.

The men took advantage of the exercise to comment entertainingly on the judicial system, which they considered to be corrupt. They brought up issues of rehabilitation and the difficulties involved with getting work after being in prison. Discussions followed about money issues, the arguments at home and the escalation towards violence. Money issues led to the topic of how difficult it is to get work as an ex-con and how all that is available to them is illegal work – how everyone has a mate down the pub who could set them up with such work. However two storylines emerged that made a significant and lasting impact on the group.

In the first, the son and daughter ended up in the centre of the circle. Peter, the man playing the daughter, was an exceptionally good actor – a creative risk-taker who had already had exchanges with other characters including both the parents in the exercise. Peter had asked the father why he never came to any of 'her' school dancing recitals and why he constantly broke his promises to take 'her' out. His insistence as the little girl had been very power-ful, rendering the father (played by the actor from the play) speechless. In conversations with the mother, Peter asked why his father hit her and why the mother allowed him to.

The inmate playing the son, Gareth, had been the first to volunteer. He later told us that he had no idea what the exercise was going to ask of him, but he had learned in prison to volunteer first and get it over and done with. The nature of the exercise required him to constantly return to his role and he handled this well despite his initial discomfort. Suddenly Gareth was faced with his little sister, played by Peter, in the centre of the circle. 'She' began to tell him how scared she was of their father, asking why their parents were always fighting, why their father hit their mother. Gareth stood in silence through this barrage of questions, eyes fixed on the ground. The little sister continued to plead with him for explanations and ended with her begging her big brother Gareth to protect her from their father if he ever tried to hurt her. At this Gareth hunched down with his head in his hands. The little sister con-tinued relentlessly. Suddenly Gareth stood up and signalled a time out. He turned to Peter and apologised, saying it was nothing personal about working with him (a necessary explanation in a prison setting). I signalled for him to leave the circle and for another to enter to maintain the momentum of the exercise and take attention away from Gareth.

Gareth stepped out of the circle and headed to the toilets, accompanied by a guard. On his return, he spoke with another member of the team, drank some water and then insisted on returning to the exercise. When the exercise finished, Gareth asked if he could address the group. He told us that he had found himself suddenly transported back to being a child trying to protect his siblings from his abusive father. He spoke of his father's temper and violent attacks which he, as the eldest child, suffered the most. For the first time Gareth had realised that his children were now going through the same experiences because of his own actions. His children were probably asking the same questions and living in fear of his mood swings. Gareth could not believe that he had become his father. He was shocked that he could have forgotten what it was like to be the child of an abusive parent. Before that moment he had never seen a link with his adult behaviour. 'How do I comfort the scared child that was me, when I've become the monster I know he's so scared of?' he asked.

The second incident arose when the husband confronted his own father in the circle. The father was played by inmate Ian, the husband (Paul) by the actor who had performed the play. Top dog Ian was always the man most in control of his emotions, the most eloquent and educated speaker and a very active participant. I am sure that had Ian not been such a willing participant in the workshops, it would have affected the willingness of many of the men. He commanded and got respect and it was clear that he was feared. It was Ian's masterful control of his temper and emotions that gave a sense of him being potentially more dangerous than the other prisoners; as if that tight control could explode at any moment and all hell would break loose when it did.

While I knew what the men in the group had been imprisoned for, I did not have specific information on each individual to link to a particular sentence. Although the information was available to us, I did not want it. I knew the nature of the offences committed by those in the group because this was rele-vant to my preparation, but I saw no gain in associating any individual with a particular crime. It could lead to subconsciously labelling and judging them; it also takes away the voice I try to give these people through my work. Over the course of the workshops the men shared a lot of information directly and indirectly which left little unknown, but it was their choice to tell what they told and the power to do so stayed with them. Ian was the most guarded. He had shared a significant amount of his story but had done so with care and calculation.

The actor playing Paul met in the circle with Ian playing his father. As the con-versation developed, Paul asked why his father had hit his mother when he was a child. The father calmly denied this, saying Paul was a liar or had imagined it. Paul persisted, becoming more agitated. Ian as the father con-tinued to calmly deny the abuse. Finally Paul shouted at the father that he used to watch from the stairs through the banister and had seen his father hit his mother. Ian too became agitated but said nothing. Paul continued to describe the scenes he had watched through the banister at the top of the stairs. Enraged, Ian suddenly yelled, 'You did not see it. The door was closed! You did not see it!' The circle gasped at the significance of his words and the latent admission of guilt that lay behind them.

Ian was clearly upset. He talked about his choice of words afterwards, saying he couldn't keep denying his actions, but he needed to deny to himself that there had been a witness to the abuse, especially his child. The men talked about what it meant to know that their children had witnessed them being abusive. Acts of violence in front of the children and turning on a child were, they unanimously agreed, lines it was unacceptable to cross.

It became evident that there were issues that needed attention within the work that could no longer be ignored. To bring the project to a close, the men prepared a performance of their own where they opted to each present a memory from the past, present, and one they wished to create for the future. Some did so by presenting scenes, others used images and some gave mono-logues in a talking heads format. Through this performance they shared their stories, new understandings and their hopes that things can change.

Most of the men went on to an obligatory prison programme to encourage better behaviour on the outside. The prison told us there was a marked dif-ference between the men on the programme who had worked with us and those who hadn't. They found the former not only more cooperative, but able to process their thoughts and feelings better. As a result we have now esta-blished an ongoing relationship with the prison, tying in our work with their programmes. Despite our workshops being voluntary, they continue to enjoy full subscription.

Women's perspectives

With one particular women's group who participated in the early stages of our domestic abuse project, I faced participation problems from the beginning, although not with the women themselves. Before we began, I discussed ex-tensively what the workshops would entail and the purpose behind them with the caseworkers at the safety unit the women attended. I clarified the participatory nature of the work and how the group would steer the direction we took in the workshops. Everything seemed clear and guidelines for work-ing practice were laid out.

In the first workshop, two of the caseworkers insisted on being present in order to see our work. I made clear that I had no problem with this, but that they would have to participate as part of the group as otherwise participants would feel they were being watched or even tested. This can be a serious problem when the participants have low self-esteem and are victims of abuse. With this agreed, the workshop began and immediately the case-workers insisted they would only work with each other in any group or partnering exercise and would only participate in the exercises they chose to. This behaviour created a rift which I decided to ignore for the first workshop, as I believed drawing attention to it at this stage risked further division.

As the day proceeded aspects came to light that required me to keep adapting both the exercises and my approach. The women in the group were survivors of domestic abuse. All had left an abusive relationship and moved on with their lives; however many now had a new partner who was also abusive. The caseworkers considered the group meetings a success, yet many of the women had been attending the group for several years and, although free of the relationship that had originally brought them there, they were clearly not free of its effects. When certain exercises were proposed the caseworkers intervened before the women could respond, saying that they thought it would be uncomfortable to talk about their relationships. They suggested that the group look at issues other than domestic abuse and its effects. The caseworkers did not see their behaviour as oppressive, yet they prevented the women from speaking up for themselves. What they viewed as protective behaviour was unhelpful and counterproductive, as it stopped the women talking about what had brought them to the group in the first place.

The women themselves seemed uncertain and explained that they did not actually discuss their relationships in their group, but instead tried to talk of happy things. For the last few years they had been talking about any subject other than the one they were supposedly there for. As I pushed on and we delved into some exercises the women got upset. This is not unusual in applied theatre work which often deals with sensitive issues and where the rule is always to let the person work through their emotion.

If someone cries it is customary to rush to comfort them, because their emotion makes us uncomfortable. Unfortunately it stops the person dealing with the emotion that has arisen in them, because their embarrassment and discomfort take over and the processing phase is hampered. Our reaction to another's distress is usually more about ourselves than about them. In this workshop, each time a woman showed any emotion, a caseworker intervened and took her out of the room. This disrupted the group. And by taking the women away, they shamed them by implying that they could not cope and should not behave emotionally in front of others. It also prevented the women from showing their feelings within the group, as if emotions should not be shown publicly. This message is completely contrary to how I work and teach. Such actions nurtured dependence by these women on the caseworkers which prevented their taking action themselves to deal with the issues they were facing.

Funding for the centre was dependent on numbers and the fact that these women attended the centre and had done so for years was viewed as a success. Nobody asked how their issues were being dealt with or what progress had been made. Nobody questioned why these women were, after five years, still unable to discuss their past relationships, why their self-esteem was still so low, or why some had embarked on new relationships in which they were again experiencing abuse. I asked the caseworkers how they dealt with the women's low self-esteem and victim mentality. The response was that the women attended classes about doing their hair and make-up, a massage class to help with relaxation and another to look at clothes and how to dress. All the funding was being used to focus on their superficial external image, while their internal problems, the reasons why they had ended up in this unit, were ignored. The women were basically being told that if they fixed their appearance, their lives would improve. I couldn't help but see similarities between their treatment by the centre and by their abusive partners.

When we began working with the group we thought the caseworkers shared our goals. But whereas our work encouraged empowerment and independence, which would hopefully leave the women no longer needing to attend the group or could help them to mentor women in similar positions, the centre operated a system of avoidance and dependence. It became clear that if the caseworkers were there, we would have no freedom to develop the project. Our theatre workshops were fine as entertainment but I could not engage the group in an applied theatre project.

We made the difficult decision to withdraw. In further talks with the caseworkers, it became evident that they did not want us to explore or even broach the topic of domestic abuse. For us, this made the project redundant. They argued that they were uncomfortable with seeing the women upset and having to deal with topics that made them uncomfortable. A domestic abuse project exploring the topic with victims of that abuse will naturally be uncomfortable and give rise to emotional responses. Unable to agree on an approach, it was clear that the project the case workers sought was not the one we could offer.

Victim turning on victim

In the safety units in the UK set up to deal with domestic abuse, there has been controversy over the use of the terms 'victim' and 'survivor' to describe those who have been subjected to abuse. Many find the word victim debilitating. Among the groups I have worked with, it became increasingly clear that it is for the women themselves to determine the discourse. The distinction they made was that if they were still with the abusive partner they were victims; if they had left and tried to move on with their lives, they were survivors. This distinction was crucial to how the women viewed themselves, but also to how they viewed and even judged one another.

With most groups I jump into the games with little introduction or discussion. I want to play with their expectations and perceptions of what applied theatre is going to be. I don't want to give them too much time to think. That way, I get a truer grasp of their uncontrived reaction and body language. If they over-process the topic of the project and their situation as victims, they become self-conscious whereas if they are trying to get their heads around an exercise, they focus on it and do not feel they are being observed by others in the group or the project facilitators. Working in a women's safety unit, starting with games was the best way to relax the women and show them it was not about getting things 'right'.

Safety units offer women who have been abused a comprehensive range of services through domestic abuse or rape, from support and counselling, to helping take a case to court. All sixteen women in the group before me came from abusive relationships – some had left their partners, others were still with them. Being there acknowledged that they had a problem and needed support, even if they were as yet unable to leave the abusive relationship. Most women in safety units have low self-esteem and believe they are stupid – having usually been told so incessantly by their partners – and fear rebuke if they make a mistake. At the start of the project many are afraid that they may make a mistake or not understand what is asked of them. The games relieve that tension and introduce laughter and fun. We, the facilitating team, make a point of joining in, showing how we too can become confused and make mistakes and that it is not about getting it right or wrong.

After an opening game, I introduced the women to the idea of the play *'Til death do us part*. I explained the storyline and we discussed what they might find upsetting in the play. Unlike the workshops with the men, I asked the women to create the life of the husband and wife in the play before they saw it. It was important for these women that they knew what to expect. I asked questions about the kind of behaviour we could expect from the wife when the husband became abusive and the typical comments she might make when tensions were rising. Only then did the women watch the play, knowing they could request a time out at any point they felt uncomfortable. I observed them nodding in acknowledgement, shaking their heads in sympathy and commenting quietly to one another. But I did not expect the response that followed.

When the play ended, I asked the women what they thought and felt about it. Immediately and unanimously they began to criticise the wife, blaming her for the abuse, berating her for being weak and stupid, claiming she enjoyed being a victim. I realised I had to change tack to deal with this negative and abusive reaction. Alarmed that the women were in denial about their own situation, I decided to do an image exercise. I asked them to take turns at moulding the husband into images representative of him being abusive and then to mould the wife into her response. In every image the wife was moulded to look weak, pathetic and insignificant. I asked the women to call out words to describe the wife and all were derogatory: stupid, pathetic, ugly, idiot. The women had turned into their abusers. In work of this kind it is not uncommon for the oppressed to turn into the oppressor. It is part of a denial process that has to be acted out before the participant is willing to look more closely at themselves.

I then asked the women each to replace the wife and take on a position that represented how they would react in the same situation. They found themselves taking on similar, if not identical, positions to those they had moulded for the wife. In each case I asked what they saw in the image. Initially the women continued their denial, ignoring the positions they had taken, but slowly began to see the similarities. They spoke about how they did not want to see themselves as weak and powerless, as they had viewed the wife in the play. They explained that, as a victim of abuse, you spend much of your time in denial. You want to believe that you aren't in that position, that you have not allowed this to happen to you. You want to believe the promises that it will never happen again and you don't want to accept that you are a victim. They told me the play had confronted them with images of their own denial and that is what they disliked and why they had disliked the wife. She was proof of the lie they told themselves, the lie that their situation was different, the lie that they were not a victim. One woman said:

> At first when I started coming to the safety unit I thought I was different from all the other women. I told them I wasn't a victim. I could walk away from the abuse at any time. That's what you keep telling yourself but the truth is you aren't any different, and you don't walk away.

These admissions were significant but I knew we had to do a follow up exercise that gave the women a chance to engage with the victim they were acknowledging themselves to be. Only in that way could they come to see a way forward and not be stuck feeling hopeless because of this recognition of themselves. I chose an exercise I call Significant Ages, in which each woman thinks of five significant periods in their life – possibly something that happened in childhood, a moment of teenage rebellion, even a marriage. They then take turns as protagonist to mould five others into static positions representing themselves at each of the points they have chosen. With this complete, the protagonist passes from one to the next, speaking to her, offering advice, warnings, encouragement, whatever is relevant to the age and event that marked that period for that woman, while the statues stay frozen and unresponsive.

After this procedure, the statues can ask the protagonist questions, request further clarification or even challenge her. Although they can now speak, the statues cannot move and they have to work hard to get the attention of the protagonist when all are free to talk at the same time. Afterwards, they discuss the version of themselves each was most drawn to and why, which ones they avoided, which ones surprised them. One woman, Janet, moulded herself as a child who lost her father when she was eight, a teenager trying to fit in with the popular group, marrying her husband in her twenties, a couple of years later when she was hit for the first time and, finally, at the birth of her first child. As she spoke to each one she began to mourn the loss of her father, realising that through her husband she had sought the safety she felt she had lost when her father died. But when the eight-year-old statue questioned her, it was revealed that her father used to beat her mother. This was a fact Janet had completely forgotten and she was shocked to realise that she had placed herself in the same situation years later. Janet tried to guide her younger self not to be so desperate to fit in; she advised her against marrying her husband, tried to convince herself to leave him after the first beating and scolded herself for not leaving after her child was born.

Nearly all the women moulded a statue of themselves at the moment they were first beaten and each spoke to the statue with great compassion. They reasoned with her about why she should leave and countered their own arguments and longing to believe that he would change. Many of the women insisted their husbands had never hit their children and that if he had she would have left him. Yet the exercise revealed many had been beaten while pregnant and the statues challenged them on this point – remember, the statues were other women from the group – claiming they had therefore endangered their children.

In addition to the realisations they made through interacting with the statues, each woman was also working on the issue while being the statues. The questions they asked, the challenges they made and their compliance with certain situations, opened up the topic in a way they could manage. Even the quietest members of the group became immersed in the exercise and found a strong voice that demanded to be heard. At the end of the exercise the women asked if they could mould the statues again and choose the one they most empathised with to embrace. I was surprised by this suggestion but could see that the women felt it was necessary and so it was essential for us to include. Every woman without exception chose herself as a child to embrace, comforting her and promising that life could be different.

Plays and performances

Applied theatre is theatre nonetheless, and should be engaging and entertaining for both participant and spectator. It is the role of the facilitator/writer to ensure that the theatricality is never lost. Only in this way will people believe in what they see and be willing to partake in the applied theatre journey. Sometimes applied theatre focuses solely on a project; sometimes the final outcome is a performance; in some projects a play is used as a starting point to introduce the issues to be dealt with in the project which will follow; sometimes the play is designed to open an interrogatory process, sometimes it may even be used to provoke.

The facilitator may be helping the group to create a piece, or taking the stories of others to write a scenario to be used as a professional piece of theatre. *'Til death do us part* was written from the stories of others, with the intention of provoking discussion on the issue of domestic abuse. During the project the play was used for a variety of purposes to serve the needs of the group being worked with. It was generally used as an introduction to the project, to open up discussion on a topic the participants were uncomfortable with or considered taboo. In working with perpetrators the play was used as a balanced introduction to the subject matter and an invitation to participate in the workshops that would follow. Because the play did not take sides or concern itself with good versus evil, the perpetrators did not feel judged or threatened and perceived that they were being sympathised with or that they were in some way justified in their actions. Of course such a reaction required selective viewing and the play did not allow for a one-sided view to be sustained, though it did try to step back from judgement. Most importantly it opened the door for discussions on perception and how we use perception to justify our actions and blame others.

The play enabled us to examine different perceptions and reasons for behaviour with a view to affecting future reactions and behaviour patterns without making participants feel defensive or angry. Invoking antagonism would render a project impossible. For victim/survivor groups the play was usually performed in the latter stages of the project when the group themselves determined the outcome of the play. The ending would be tested and rewritten within the context of what had been learned as the project proceeded. For example after seeing the play, participants would have a chance to discuss other possible outcomes and the factors that might influence these outcomes. The participants would have the opportunity to question the characters and experiment with them and their possible choices. The end of the play could then be altered in response to the participants' explorations.

When 'Til Death do us Part was shown to the general public to stimulate discussion and debate over an issue prevalent throughout society, the early responses were defensive. The audience said they found the husband witty and entertaining, and that while they sympathised with what had happened to the wife they had found it difficult to connect with her and her choices because they found her frustrating, even contradictory. Initial reactions to the performance were thus about acknowledging that while there may be an issue of right and wrong, our reactions are not black and white since people are not all good or all bad. Audiences quickly made analogies with their own relationships with parents, siblings, work colleagues or even friends. It was clear that conflict is not limited to a husband and wife situation such as in the play, and that behavioural patterns in conflict relationships are similar, whatever that relationship might be.

As an applied theatre project, this was a rich starting ground as it immediately brought us into the field of perception. It enabled us to look at how we interpret things in light of our own reactions, knowledge and emotions; how at times we see things as we desire them to be rather than as they are, because it reinforces our own sense of righteousness or security. This applies also to how we hear things and selectively retain things heard, or change the tone with which they were originally said to alter intent and meaning; the way we hear things that were never actually said.

The design of the work and the steps taken to build these plays ensure that the participants work in a safe environment. It is this safe environment that allows participants to explore sensitive issues and ensure that relationships always feel real. Theatre allows safety and protection from the immediacy of the issue, while being real enough for the investigation into it to take place in a believable way.

Reflections

Applied theatre is a developing field, encompassing new practices and old. So it is constantly experimenting and developing, resisting classification or the notion that there is a right or wrong way to go about it. I have found that evaluation tools such as project write-ups can help us learn from one another and increase knowledge within the field by sharing our experience and our awareness that many projects are experimental in nature. As a team working on different issues across different countries, we have learned the importance of sharing the lessons we have learned, often the hard way, from each project.

Applied theatre work never formally ends. It is complete for us as facilitators at a certain stage, but we hope that the work continues through its influence on the individual or community. Since the work always belongs to those we have been working with, to try to draw definitive conclusions about its success or failure when your time with the project is complete appears to ignore the participatory nature which is so essential to the work.

In the US prison I changed the planned exercises after seeing the reaction of the men to the play. In circumstances of that kind I am making one intuitive decision after another about how the project will best advance and I depend upon my team to work with those sudden decisions and changes because there is no time to discuss and re-plan. With my own teams this is well established and we readily adapt easily to one another. We know the overall plan and that there are good reasons for any changes we introduce. We also know the importance of responding immediately to those changes as a team, not showing uncertainty or confusion. I know the team trust that I make the changes because they are in the best interests of the group we are working with. I know I don't have to take them aside and explain my decisions, although we discuss changes and why they occurred in extensive reflection meetings afterwards. Working with a new team as the project initiator or consultant is quite different.

In the prison my change of plan caught the team off guard, although we had discussed the importance of moving with the group and their responses. The actors, who were also trained facilitators, initially looked uncertain, although they quickly adapted to the new exercise. With this team the change in exercises still related to exercises we had discussed and planned: the change was in the order and in how we approached the exercise. I spent a lot of time working with them beforehand so we could become accustomed to the way each of us worked and build on the trust that is so essential to the work. We had gone through most of the exercises the men in the prison would undertake. Any crack in the facilitating team can severely affect the project and make it more about the facilitators than about the people we work with.

Care also has to be taken over words used to describe the groups we work with. We have always referred to the domestic abuse project as a project which looks at conflict in relationships. This is so that people do not feel labelled or judged. In the prison settings the men are often extremely defensive at the start and a poor choice of words can immediately alienate them. I make a point of explaining to groups in prisons that I am not there to judge them – they have already been judged and that is why they are in prison. I am not interested in judging further nor do I want to know what anyone is in prison for. Instead my goal, I explain, is to work together to explore things like behaviour, perception and action.

Working with commissioning agents can bring complications. When the goals of the team and the agent are clearly at odds the project generally needs to be revised and a decision made on whether or not it should go ahead. When staff or agents wish to be present certain guidelines have to be laid down and adhered to. I encourage staff to be present, as the project can be a learning opportunity for them about the people with whom they work. In a prison setting staff are there in a policing role and this must be accepted as a legal requirement for the project to occur. At times I encourage staff to participate as equal members of the workshop but such decisions must be taken carefully and be sensitive to the make-up of the group. Inviting staff to join in prison workshops can shut down open discussion. In the women's groups, staff sitting watching them but not participating can make the women feel uneasy that they are being watched and judged.

We are similarly careful how we select moments for the facilitating team to participate in a game or exercise. Participation removes a 'them and us' scenario at times, but at others it can create discomfort in the group and unwillingness to participate. Every project, every exercise and every game is about balance. It's about finding the right balance among all the people involved and enabling an atmosphere of growth and cooperation in the process.

Principles and practice

- Incorporate a time out procedure to allow participants the opportunity to take a break if they are feeling overwhelmed
- Trust the methods to work even when you are thrown curve balls
- Avoid giving advice or telling people how to act. Let them make their own decisions in their own time – exercises should be designed to help people make realisations for themselves following a period of guided exploration
- Applied theatre is a developing field and so there is scope for experimentation within the work
- There must be a trust in the facilitating team that all have each other's back
- In reflection meetings afterwards discuss changes to the proposed plan and explain why they were made
- Take care over words used to describe the group. Avoid terminology that labels them
- Working with commissioning agents can bring complications if the goals of the team and the agent are at odds
- Do not be afraid to withdraw from a project when there is discordance with the commissioning agent
- If staff ask to participate they should do so as equal members of the workshop. Decisions about this must be taken carefully and show sensitivity towards the group to ensure discussion is not shut down. The participation of staff can remove a 'them and us' scenario but equally it can create discomfort in the group and unwillingness to participate

5

African trails

'Run!' I was commanded, as a handful of people came tearing past, looking terrified. I didn't move. 'Run!' Abdi shouted again, turning angrily to see why I wasn't following. 'Why?' I asked, determined not to budge without good reason. Abdi couldn't hide his irritation. 'What do you mean why? Are you crazy? Just run Jennifer! Run!'

Over a decade of working on applied theatre projects has taught me to act with caution. I have a tendency to find myself in the wrong place at the wrong time. Working with gangs and problem youth, I have also learned that a command to run usually means the police are in hot pursuit or, worse, a rival gang. I know that at times it is better to stand still and let the rush pass by, along with who or whatever is in pursuit, thus showing that I am not a part of it. This, as it turned out, was not one such occasion.

I should have known that in Africa a command to run should always be heeded. It could mean anything – a wild animal on the loose... armed bandits moving in for an attack... Better to run first and explain later if it turns out to be the police or military although, even in those cases, it is often better to just keep going. You will never hear a command to run if it's a life threatening insect or reptile, so it's safe to assume that you are being told to run for a very good reason. Unfortunately one too many sticky situations have led me to ask questions when all that is required is action.

Abdi glowered at me, furious. 'Never mind. It's too late now.' I looked at him confused. He was facing me, which meant I had my back to the direction from which he had come running. 'Don't move. Just stand very still no matter what. Can you manage that?' he asked a little too sarcastically, adding 'It will all be over soon.' Abdi's words turned the look of confusion on my face to one of horror. What did he mean? Was I about to die? Slowly, against his advice, I turned to look behind me and confront my fate. What I saw resembled a carpet being rolled out in my direction, at incredible speed. Only as it drew closer did I realise it was rats, thousands upon thousand of rats.

I stood there uncertain whether to keep my eyes open or closed. I was fascinated by the sight before me, yet repulsed and horrified at the same time. Abdi explained that, if we stayed still, the pack of rats would soon pass and that I should ignore them if they sniffed around and investigated me for a while. Easier said than done. Over the next few minutes, literally thousands of rats ran past me, some stopping to investigate, their cold wet noses burrowing under my trousers. I cringed as I felt them against my skin, forcing myself not to look down or run. Not that there was anywhere to run to, and any move-ment would only have harnessed their attention. 'Stop making so much noise.' Abdi hissed at me. I glared back at him and hissed back between gritted teeth, 'I'm whimpering you idiot. It's called fear!' 'Well rats are sensitive to sound so shut up!' I wanted to kill him. Abdi was my Zimbabwean co-facilitator for workshops based on looking at ways of dealing with oppression, and all I could think about was the multiple ways I would like to end his life, all of them entailing excessive violence.

In the first year I worked in Africa I learned that I was going to have to deal with rats everywhere. In workshops they scurried around the floor while we worked, and at night I listened to the sound of them scratching at the roof above and dodged them if I had to get up in the dark. At first I did as most people would. I screamed. I ran. I jumped on chairs, tables or any nearby sur-face. But as time went on I learned the futility of all these measures. Scream-ing has no effect, a rat can outrun me every time and, despite all cartoons to the contrary, standing on chairs is futile because rats can climb and they can swim – who knew that?

I have also learned – never mind how – to always look down the toilet before sitting on it! I learned that hungry rats will feed on soft cartilage. The notion that they will sniff and run depends greatly on their hunger and, apparently, geographical location. Basically, I learned that everything I thought I knew about rats was wrong.

TVO branches out into Africa

In 2007 TVO branched out to begin projects in Africa. With new territory came new projects and new understandings. One project led to another as news of our work spread, and each year we found ourselves venturing into new countries on the continent. Some African projects were sponsored by commissioning agents, others were work we felt strongly about getting involved in, despite lack of funds. We have received occasional grants to fund us through our work in Africa, in particular in the refugee camp in Uganda. However the African work is largely supported through fundraising and generous donations from the public.

Africa was a new adventure but it came with new difficulties and was a world for which we were unprepared. Fear, corruption, military oppression, even witchcraft were not new, most being significant features when I worked in South America. However disease, rats, bats and other unwelcome insect and wildlife, cultural norms, bandits, and government resistance were some of the problems that came our way in Africa. In some countries we have even had to deal with people's fears that they will be punished by the government if they work with us. This is why we haven't changed our name from the mouthful that is Theatre versus Oppression. We often get easier access to groups and are dismissed more easily by governments or ruling bodies because they think we are 'just actors'. There are areas where we have worked that we would never have had access to if they had seen us as anything other than performers.

In Zimbabwe, however, the name of our organisation caused a problem. We were told to avoid using the words 'oppressed' and 'oppression' in our work. Considering our organisation is called Theatre versus Oppression and our workshops were looking at different kinds of oppression, this proved challenging. We were officially renamed in Zimbabwe as Theatre for Healing. Our work in the refugee camp in Uganda requires permission papers to be issued by the Ugandan government or we can be forcibly removed from the camp. To date, nobody has ever asked us for these papers but were we caught without them we would be in trouble. Every visit to the camp requires a lengthy visit to the camp commander and other officials as a courtesy and an act of expected respect. Vaccinations, malaria medication and jigger checks form part of our annual preparations. A jigger is a flea that burrows into the sole of your foot and lays its eggs, killing all the flesh around it as it grows. But they are fairly harmless if caught early and can be dug out with a safety pin.

When TVO puts a team together for a project we must first weigh up the situation and be sure the facilitators will be safe. With our work in Africa that has been complex. We cannot guarantee that the team will not become ill, even with malaria medication and precautions. We stay in poor conditions for the duration of the project each year, living in the refugee camp, where the jiggers thrive. In other African countries, I have conducted workshops with rats scurrying around me. We have been attacked by bandits in Uganda, robbed in Kenya, had a herd of cattle stampede a workshop in Tanzania and we have been threatened in too many places to list here. Often people have a glamorous concept of what our work entails but the reality is that we often work in extremely difficult and unpleasant circumstances.

So we must always calculate the dangers involved and ensure that the team are aware of the risks and equipped to deal with them. We try to have both male and female facilitators on the team but this is not always feasible or acceptable. We also try to ensure that the facilitating team has a cultural mix. Volunteer staff who have trained with and work for TVO are currently based in eight different countries so we have managed fairly often to create the desired mix. With each project we try to ensure there is a range of expertise, usually decided by the demands of the project, and also a range of cultural backgrounds and language abilities.

This chapter looks at three projects – in Tanzania, Kenya and Uganda, to give an overall view of the varied work we have done. The first two were one-off projects, put together for a specific issue at a specific time. Tanzania, was a training event rather than a project, where people from around the country were brought together to be trained in the use of applied theatre in their communities. The Kenya project was a project designed to address a specific issue, tribal unrest and violence during elections in 2010 within a conference setting.

Uganda, however, is one of our few ongoing projects. We return to work on it annually and have invested a great deal in it. After our first year in Uganda we made a commitment to develop the project work there indefinitely and, in the process, to create an applied theatre group based in the refugee camp. We also committed ourselves to help build a school and support the creation of a women's safety unit.

Tanzania

In 2007 TVO was invited by a European organisation working with global justice issues to run a training programme in Tanzania. They had heard about the training we had been doing in Zimbabwe and were keen to set up a similar programme through the projects they supported in Tanzania. Their plan was to fund a two-week intensive training course, bringing me in from the UK to run it, supported by one of their staff members.

The group being trained were formed from representatives of the twenty-six regions of Tanzania. They were brought to a central location to work on applied theatre techniques, and determine how the stories from their community could be openly discussed and learned from. We worked especially with the topic of HIV/AIDS, which had personally affected them all, as well as their communities.

I had been working on various projects in Africa, principally Zimbabwe, and had quickly learned that time keeping and attendance were tricky issues in communities where people had so many demands upon them and so little personal time. The appeal of this project was, in part, the fact that we would be taken to an isolated location for its duration ensuring, I believed somewhat naively, perfect attendance and excellent time keeping.

The day before the workshops began everyone started arriving from all over the country, many with no more than a toothbrush for luggage. We were staying in a remote lodge. Back in the UK people congratulated me on my good fortune in staying in an African lodge in the heart of Tanzania – clearly none of them had any idea what it was like. The nearest town was a four-hour walk away and we had no transport. My room was sparse, the shower had only cold water, the mosquito net had holes big enough to fit my head through and in the corner of my room, which looked out onto the bar, there was a giant hole in the wall where an air conditioning unit was supposed to be. But since working in the refugee camp in Uganda, I know that this accommodation was actually luxury.

The plan was to have intense daily workshops over a two-week period, culminating in a series of forum style performances depicting issues that affected the day-to-day lives in the villages the groups had come from. The project ran into problems before the workshops even began. The participants were horrified to discover that they had each been booked into separate rooms. While a westerner might welcome space and privacy, the Tanzanians found this arrangement solitary and anti-social. Within half an hour they had rearranged themselves into groups of three or four per room, sharing the one double bed. The lodge, while pleased at an arrangement that freed up more than half the booked rooms, did not miss the opportunity to make a quick buck, and insisted all the rooms had been booked and would have to be paid for.

The lodge was to provide breakfast, lunch and dinner, as well as catering for two breaks where we would be served tea and biscuits. This was far more food than most of our participants were accustomed to. The menu changed daily, so they could try foods they would not otherwise encounter, especially meat.

For me, a vegetarian, the cook seemed capable of making only one dish. After the first week of being served the same meal for lunch and dinner, I spoke to the cook and we talked about the many and varied dishes he could make with the ingredients available. He nodded enthusiastically and proposed a number of dishes himself. That night I arrived at the dining hall to find the same meal I had been eating for the last seven days. When I asked the cook what had happened, he apologised and assured me the next day would be different. It wasn't.

The two tea breaks were chaotic. The participants worked on the premise of first come first served. Those at the front of the queue helped themselves to all the heated milk and as many biscuits as they could fit in one hand. The rest were lucky to get a cup of black coffee or tea. The charge to the break table was something to behold. We would be mid-workshop when the hotel staff began laying everything out. The group would wait impatiently for me to announce that it was break time. I had to move fast and get in line first if I wanted milk for my tea, or move to the side before the stampede ploughed me down. As the days progressed, I learned to edge slowly towards the table during the workshop. Only when I was in front of it would I announce that it was break time, ensuring I was first in line. If you can't beat them as they say... In Africa you quickly learn the futility of insisting on better organisation – everyone will agree and make promises and nothing happens. Or worse, nobody will understand what your problem is!

Those attending the workshop ranged in age from eighteen to mid-sixties and were from poor villages around the country. The commissioning organisation was keen for the project to educate about HIV/AIDS being spread through sexual activity, as statistics showed that the numbers of Tanzanians with AIDS was escalating. The problem was further confounded by the increase in prostitution and the fact that sex with a prostitute was more expensive if the client requested to use a condom, even if he provided his own.

Each participant was to receive a small stipend and their transport money, which the commissioning agent unwisely decided to pay on arrival. The first morning I went to the lodge's conference to begin the workshops, only to find myself alone. It turned out that all the participants had drunk the small bar on the premises dry the night before. This explained – belatedly – the noise in the bar through the night, clearly audible through the large hole in my wall (through which the participants frequently came to see what I was doing) and where they played the same three songs endlessly day and night for the two weeks. I called the organisation in charge to say that the participants had spent all the money they had been given – their stipend and expenses for the journey home. They did not seem bothered saying this was 'normal' and at least no one could go off anywhere now. This was not the encouraging response I had hoped for. By the time I got the group together in the work room that afternoon, many were still drunk and the rest severely hung over.

When we finally started the workshops I found that the commissioning organisation had decided that as many in the group spoke no English, the two most fluent English speakers in the group (I use the word 'fluent' loosely) would take shifts as the official translators. This was the first time I was in a situation where I could not speak the language and was dependent on others. Even working in countries where I was not fluent in the language, another member of the facilitating team usually was and, with our intuitive understanding of one another and our approaches to the work, translation was quite straightforward.

I stood in front of the group and explained who I was, why I was there and how happy I was to have the opportunity to work with them. Then I turned to my translator to allow him to translate what I had just said. He was silent. I looked at him and he stared back blankly. 'Aren't you going to translate?' I asked. 'No,' came the blunt response. "What? Why not?' 'We know who you are and why you are here. I'll translate when you say something worth translating.' Clearly this was not going to be easy.

Over the next two weeks I came to appreciate the true meaning of 'lost in translation'. Often I would speak briefly but the translation would take ten times longer, or the reverse would happen. I had no way of knowing what was being translated, or how, and it rapidly became clear that my translators were both selective and subjective. If they thought there was a better way to do something, or didn't like what I said, they believed it was their right to change it, usually without warning me. They would begin an activity and then not follow an instruction I had given. When I queried this I was told by my translator that he had not given it because he didn't like it. Or a translation would cause hilarity in the group when I had said nothing funny.

At first I felt frustrated and annoyed that the group had no respect for me or the work. My supposed assistant from the commissioning organisation left immediately after dropping me off, leaving contact numbers but making it clear that her assistance did not stretch beyond that and the occasional visit to see how things were progressing. I felt utterly alone, especially as nobody would sit at my table during meal times and would even move elsewhere if I tried to sit with them. After spending the first couple of days feeling hurt, annoyed and indignant, I realised that I was turning what was happening into being all about me. In truth, it had nothing to do with me but was a way for the group to reinforce their individuality and sense of self-worth when they felt devalued because a white person had been brought in to tell them how to work with their communities. Instead of feeling sorry for myself, I had to look at the group and work out how I could address what was causing this reaction, how I could return their sense of self-worth and show them we were working together, that there was no scale of superiority. I needed them to understand they all had something to offer and we were looking for ways to share that.

The purpose of this project was to serve as a training event, to teach some basic Theatre of the Oppressed, improvisation and reflection techniques. The group were to return home and use these skills to deal with sensitive issues in their community. The methods were intended to encourage an interactive approach with the village communities, helping them see how applied theatre techniques could be used to tackle sensitive, even taboo, topics in an entertaining way that engaged the community. The people gathered for the training all had a leadership role within their communities, but the training, although intensive, was brief when one considered the high expectations of how it would be followed through. Many of the group also felt undermined by being told they had to learn these methods and would be tested on them by the commissioning agent, who would travel to their communities to check up on how they were implementing what they had learned. I realised if we were to advance at the requisite speed and at the same time establish trust, I needed to tap into their own experience and find out how this could be used in an applied theatre way.

The group needed to see that I valued their experience and knowledge, and that I recognised that they had something valuable to offer. I talked about the use of games and how we use them to read situations as well as to bond the group or relieve tension, and explained how the games can be used to complement the exercises. Then I played a simple introductory game with them to illustrate how it achieved these things. I asked them to tell me about the games they had played as children and the games they used in their own work. We played these games and after each we sat and talked about how the theory of game playing could be applied to it. In this way, rather than forcing my way of doing things on them and failing to respect their own valued methods, I tried to show how the theory could be applied to their ideas and work. Be it training, a project or a performance, it has value for them to see how the culture and experience of the group can be used as applied theatre.

Nobody knows the culture or the issues better than those living it. It is they who are the experts.

The added bonus for the group is they get to teach me and watch me flounder when I don't get the game or make a mistake. In Tanzania this was not helped by the selective translations which missed out key things about the games. But it is important for the facilitating team to become participants at times and show their own vulnerability and openness to learning. I have learned much about the culture of those I worked with, what appeals to them and what is or isn't acceptable. And every African group I've worked with finds nothing more enjoyable than seeing the white person struggle or fail in a game. We are inevitably the first to be eliminated in competitive games, causing hilarity among participants, and a few bruises on our side when ejected a little too energetically.

With the Tanzanian group we advanced rapidly through the games. Each day a different person took a turn at opening and closing the workshop with their choice of game. Well, that was after a fifteen-minute prayer session that took account of the different religions in the room, and which also closed each day's work. After each game the group worked out how the theory could be applied to it. In between, I introduced exercises leading to an understanding of Boal's forum theatre, combined with his Rainbow of Desire exercises. I hoped the group would gain deeper understanding of types of oppression and how they affect each one of us. It was during an adaptation of one of these Rainbow exercises that I learned a painful lesson about properly under-standing and appreciating the different cultures I work with, and why words need to be chosen carefully and exercises adapted in light of the culture of the participants.

The exercise is entitled The Wheel of Oppression. After an in-depth discus-sion on what an oppressor is and the importance of being able to trace oppression back to a person, as opposed to an institution or concept, parti-cipants are asked to think about the oppressors in their lives. If, for example, someone names the government or religion, the concepts are too large to deal with. The oppressed person is left feeling defeated. Eventually we do build up to looking at the bigger organisation or concept but familiarity is provided by starting with a person. The group must understand that an oppressor can also be a loved one. Oppression can be the result of a particular action, a belief or an expectation someone has of you, for example, a parent who expects great intellectual success from their child, or who regularly com-pares them to a sibling. It could be the insecure spouse who is smothering their partner; or the rebellious teenager, the unsupportive or critical teacher. The point is that the oppression is not necessarily constant, though it is usually recurring, and the oppressor is not necessarily an evil person.

In the exercise, participants focus on a particular oppressor in their lives. This will usually be the person who is causing them the most difficulty at the moment. They form two concentric circles and the outer circle is asked to mould the inner into representations of their chosen oppressor. Participants are asked to focus on triggers that cause us to react to a person before they have even spoken. Triggers can be the way someone stands, the way they look or hold their head and hands, how they place their arms, even a raised eyebrow. After moulding their oppressors, the sculptors walk around looking at the different statues for points of similarity. Usually there are strong similarities among the statues and this both surprises and comforts the participants, as they realise that oppression has a similar face for all of us. In other words, even though we may each be subject to a particular oppression, we have so much in common and our issues are not as alien to one another as we tend to assume.

As the exercise proceeds, we reach a point where the sculptors begin to address their sculpted oppressors, telling them things they have perhaps always wanted to, asking questions, even challenging them. At this point the statues come alive and, armed with the knowledge gained by how they were moulded and what is being said to them, they respond as the oppressor they believe themselves to be. A conversation begins, often heated. For many, it is the only opportunity they will ever have to confront their oppressor and there is a release in doing so. For some it is about clarifying in their mind what the issue is, for others it is about gaining a different perspective. They are in a safe environment in which to challenge, question, study and afterwards discuss. Empowerment can come through realising that it is futile to confront the oppressor, seeing the situation from a different perspective, or finding a different strategy and approach to the issue. Follow up discussions and exercises deal with all of these issues.

With the Tanzanian group, we reached the point of confronting the oppressor and I gave the command for the conversations to begin. Everyone in the room immediately began to fight, throwing punches in every direction. For a brief moment I stood frozen in horror, not least at the sight of a sixty-year-old grandmother punching a man young enough to be her grandson. I screamed at them to stop, but it was futile. My voice was drowned by violent screams. Eventually I had no choice but to wade in and try to break them up, unsuccessfully dodging punches along the way. When things finally calmed down and everyone collapsed to the floor in exhaustion, I screamed at the group: 'What the hell are you doing?' My translator frowned, confused. He translated my hysterical question to the group, who were now completely calm. They stared back at me equally confused, saying in Swahili, 'You told us to confront our oppressors – this is how we confront.'

Since then I have been careful to clarify to everyone I do this exercise with that there can be no physical contact and that the confrontation is about using words and gesture. Most groups look at me as if I am crazy, not understanding why I am stating the obvious; although groups elsewhere in Africa have complained about the restriction on physical contact, insisting that it is unnatural.

The horror of witnessing the violence and knowing that I was responsible for it has stayed with me. The simple translation of the word 'confront' had created the problem: they were confounded by my lack of cultural awareness about what I was asking them to do. I realised that many of the exercises from Theatre of the Oppressed and also other practices needed to be adapted to meet the relevant cultural needs. It is easy to see an exercise work on one project and slot it into another in expectation of a similar response, but this is naïve and ignorant. The experience taught me to be more questioning of myself and the reasons why I use the exercises I do. It taught me to refrain from seeking recourse to a bank of tried and tested activities that have a general application and to trust my own intuition more, my own ability to adapt existing exercises or create my own. As long as I listened to and observed the group, I could tailor the work to their needs and what would work for them culturally, instead of assuming that my list of resources and lesson plans could stand alone.

It was a harsh and humbling lesson that cost me a black eye, swollen jaw and bloody nose!

Kenya

After the December 2007 presidential elections, Kenya found itself in a political, economic and humanitarian crisis. As Mwai Kibaki was declared president, his opponent's supporters went on a violent rampage throughout the country. Ethnic violence escalated in the Rift Valley, caught on camera for the world to see, as was the shooting of demonstrators by police. By the end of January over half a million people had been displaced. An estimated 800-1000 were killed and hundreds of others were maimed in machete attacks.

The effects of the violence have been far reaching. The fear of a repeat or escalation of the 2008 events in the 2012 election have spread throughout the country. It had been widely reported that rival factions, discontent with machetes, had begun arming themselves with AK-47s and G3 battle rifles as early as 2009, in readiness for the anticipated violence. And so in 2010 I found myself on a journey through the Rift Valley to help promote peaceful protest and tribal harmony by means of applied theatre methods. It was a TVO project working with White Fingers, a Kenyan group for the youth who were also the organisers of the event. The dates followed a visit to neighbouring Uganda, so it seemed logical to move straight on to the Kenyan project. I was no expert on tribal warfare or the background to the political unrest that took place in 2008, however. All I knew was what I saw on my TV screen, along with the rest of the world.

The journey we were to take through the spectacular Rift Valley was planned to culminate in a highly publicised conference bringing together Kenyan youth with notable public figures and politicians in a quest for peaceful co-habitation among rival tribes. My role was to visit different areas affected by the violence, attend public meetings and give talks accompanied by a group of youth delegates. I would then conduct workshops during the four-day conference, with the support of two of TVO's facilitators, leading up to a performance about issues under discussion that I would create with the participants.

Two weeks before my arrival I was informed of the performance plans and advised to read the book, *Negative ethnicity: from bias to genocide* (2003) by Kenyan academic and writer, Koigi Wa Wamwere. With the knowledge gained from reading this book, I was informed, I would be ready to put together a performance based on the pressing issues the conference would be dealing with. I managed to ignore the alarm bells ringing in my head, bought the book and began reading. Halfway into the text I realised that if I misunderstood the situation, I could be responsible for the next wave of riots in the country.

This was one of the most difficult and challenging projects I have ever undertaken: a week during which nothing went to plan, partly because no plan existed and my attempts to make one were futile, a week it seemed would never end and which resulted in some of the most ridiculous situations I have ever found myself in. None of this was helped by being attacked by bandits (see Preface) on the way to the airport in Uganda to catch a flight to Nairobi for this project. Still shaken, I was unprepared for the mayhem that Kenya unleashed upon me.

By the time we arrived at the conference location, we had already faced physical, mental and emotional challenges. One of my co-facilitators, Nelson, looked as though he had lost the will to live, thanks to four days of endless delays, changes, accidents and other problems that plagued every day of the project as we travelled around the Rift Valley with the core group of delegates. We were exhausted and frustrated. Plans to create and prepare the performance had been disbanded as the organisers decided the work should be done during the four days of the conference so the attendees could contribute to the process. Four sleepless nights, endless uncomfortable bus journeys, continual delays and painful promotional events finally ended at the conference where hundreds would gather .

The conference had been billed as a high profile event. The hall was filled with youth from all over Kenya and by representatives from other African nations, from the camps for internally displaced people (IDPs) scattered throughout the Rift Valley. The press and television were covering the conference and it was to be opened by a famous politician.

As the official start time drew close, it was clear that all was not going to plan – not unusual in itself – and we would not be starting on time. A few years of working in several countries in Africa teaches you that nothing will happen at the stated time, or any time close to it. Waiting is an art form that must be nurtured if you want to run projects successfully. Expectations of punctuality should be pushed firmly to one side. Becoming frustrated by the total disregard for time is a waste of energy and a source of immense amusement to the African hosts. As it turned out, the problem lay with the star of the conference, the famous politician, who had failed to arrive. And nothing could begin without him.

As time went by the organisers seated at a long table on the stage became more and more agitated. After a few desperate phone calls, Alfred, the president of the organisation hosting the event, approached me. He wanted me to take one of the seats on the stage. I wondered what the reasons might be for the change in plans and my elevation in status and importance. Alfred informed me that the politician who was to give the opening speech and open the conference had been called to an incident and would not be coming after all.

> Alfred: You will have to take his place and open the conference. You're not what we wanted but you'll have to do.

> Jennifer: (wondering how could I refuse such a flattering invitation) So what do I do? Do I just pronounce the conference open?

Alfred: Yes...

Jennifer: No problem, sure, I can do that.

Alfred: (nonchalantly) And give a two-hour talk.

Jennifer: What?

Alfred: Talk to the people, you have a two hour slot.

Jennifer: What? When?

Alfred: In ten minutes.

Jennifer: No! I can't talk for two hours!

Alfred: (Clearly confused by the notion that anyone could not talk for two hours and, if you have ever attended an African conference, you would understand why) What? (Irritated at my lack of cooperation) Well how long can you talk for?

Jennifer: An hour? (What was I thinking?)

Alfred: (disappointed) That's not very good, but I suppose it will have to do.

Jennifer: What am I supposed to talk about? (it hadn't occurred to me to ask this first)

Alfred: (matter-of-factly) Tribal warfare in Kenya, the violence of 2008 and the upcoming elections of 2012.

So I, one of the few white people in the room stood up in front of 300 plus people, the national press and television and spoke for one hour on the topic of tribal warfare in Kenya, the violence of 2008 and the upcoming elections of 2012. I had no idea what I was talking about and I don't know what I actually said.

The plan was that the conference participants would select which of several workshop leaders to work with, along with other participants, to study different approaches to the problems of violence and negative ethnicity. Alfred stood on stage and instructed the workshop leaders to stand at different points in the hall, and the 300 plus participants to move towards the person they wanted to work with. Within minutes I had the entire 300 plus standing in front of me. Alfred pondered the situation before asking if I thought this was unmanageable and, if so, how many I would be willing to take.

After much discussion, in which I was not included, they told me they had arrived at a solution. I was given a group of fifty and asked to begin preparing a performance with them which would be staged at a public and media-saturated event at the close of the conference. It was a large group but I had two co-facilitators, Nelson (from Paraguay) and Benson (from DRC) who had trained and worked with me in Uganda, so the plan seemed manageable.

On the first day we explored concepts of 'negative ethnicity' and what it meant to different people. From the literature I had been given to read I knew that it was common to insult a different tribe by referring to them as a specific insect or animal. I felt they could explore this idea through image work and storytelling. We also looked at notions of storytelling, an art form in Kenya, as it is in many African countries. We identified the concepts that were unique to African storytelling, such as the exaggerated descriptions, the particular use of metaphor, simile and hyperbole; the importance of a moral at the end of the story; the storyteller being an elder, thus signifying experience and wisdom, but also how the elders often contradicted one another in the stories they told. As we explored these characteristics, we established notions of memory and how memory is handed down from generation to generation. The tendency to take this knowledge for granted has decimated storytelling in many cultures in Africa, especially in the refugee camps. Ravaged by war and famine, many have dismissed the art of storytelling as having no value in their current situation. Culture and identity can easily be lost through such decisions. Resurrecting storytelling characteristics was about exploring a form steeped in tradition, the same traditions threatened by the violence of tribalism.

My aim had been to try to find a way into a negative issue through a positive one. Negative ethnicity, the brutal attacks and killings during 2008, and the feared election violence of 2012, weighed heavily on everyone in the room. Not one person from the Rift Valley had been left untouched by the violence of 2008 and many bore the scars of savage machete attacks. That those in the room were from different tribes caused some unease. I did not want to come at the subject directly as it would provoke a negative reaction. I sought the positive through exploring the traditional art of storytelling. Everyone there shared knowledge and experience of this, uniting them regardless of their tribe.

After the first day I felt we had made significant progress. We had even discussed how the ideas of traditional storytelling could be combined with the animal and insect references and be made into a story. But my sense of achievement proved to be premature. When we went to the conference room early the next morning to meet the group, we found a new group of fifty participants. Confused and concerned, I asked Alfred what was happening. He explained that as so many people wanted to work with me, he had decided that the solution was to change the group every day. Panicked, I asked how I was supposed to create a performance when I was never working with the same people. He shrugged and said he was confident that I would find a way around it.

During the week of travelling to the conference in the Rift Valley there had been a core group of youth leaders travelling with us and I generally did some activities with them each evening. As dinner was being cooked, I had encouraged them to sit round the fire and tell me the traditional stories from their childhood. I decided to ask these youth leaders to join me as my core group to work in the sessions with us during the day, and with me alone in the evenings. This was the only way to achieve any continuity. With each day's new group we repeated the process of exploring animal and insect imagery through games and exercises, and again discussed notions of storytelling and views on negative ethnicity. Each day we would tell the new group the ideas the others had put forward for a performance story about tribalism using animals and insects. They would listen and then work on devising the next part, developing the concepts further. Each evening I worked with a few of the youth leaders to develop their characters as an elderly grandparent, telling a bedtime story to their young granddaughter. Each time I was careful to ensure we included the characteristics the groups had mentioned, as well as many of the typical sayings they had recalled.

By the close of the conference a performance of sorts was complete. The group from the final day assumed the roles of the various animals and insects while the youth leaders portrayed the grandparents telling the story. The tale was about a forest in the Rift Valley where no animals lived and the birds could no longer be heard. It told how each animal had fought for supremacy through undermining the characteristics of another, until there was violence. In the end all the animals were killed. The story was not the most original or creative, but the method of storytelling was, and it embodied all the cultural aspects and traditions of storytelling that had been identified by the many participants.

As the performance got underway I remember my mixed feelings as I stood at the back of the hall. Part of me was relieved that we had been able to achieve anything at all, and that it was almost over. But the playwright and director in me cringed at the hastily thrown together performance which was rapidly taking on a life of its own. Participants eager for a greater role were now adding in new sections as we went along, usually centred on their unwillingness to die when they were supposed to. By the time a few members of the group had begun adlibbing some musical numbers, it felt like a comedic version of *The Lion King*. I collapsed into the nearest chair with my head in my hands.

When the performance finally came to an end, having gone on twenty minutes longer than scheduled, the crowd rose to their feet in a standing ovation, much to my amazement. I peered through my fingers, astonished. Had we been watching the same play? The press enthused over it and the author of the book I had been asked to read a few weeks earlier, now the guest of honour, spoke enthusiastically about how this play should be performed in every school in the country and praised me for my keen understanding of his work. It was utterly surreal.

Afterwards I met with the youth leaders for an evaluation and reflection session. I expressed my amazement at the response the piece had received and they responded to my reaction with equal confusion. They explained that the performance had all the elements that an African audience would want in terms of entertainment, that there had been a moral to the story, laughter, music, dancing (not in the version I had directed) and that the link to tribalism and negative ethnicity had been clear. One of the boys suddenly asked me why I was so judgmental. He pointed out that I was judging the performance by my western standards and told me I had to learn to see with African eyes if I was going to work on this continent. He was right of course. My comparisons were with the plays I was accustomed to – polished, well rehearsed performances. I had come to the piece with all the expectations I believed a western audience would have, and could only see its shortcomings.

Kenya, like Tanzania, was a teaching ground for me. It was a reminder of the need to learn from the people I work with rather than, however unintentionally, enforcing my own approach or way of thinking. It has been difficult to re-adjust my notions of what a performance should be as my work in Africa has developed. I watch different groups' performances with a western director's critical eye, but then I look around at the spectators and see how they connect with the piece and invest their time and emotions into it so willingly. It reminds me that those creating the performance will always know more about the issues they deal with than I shall, that they will always understand their audience and its needs better than I ever can. I remember that though I am a teacher, I must not forget that I am also a student.

Uganda

Some time back I spent four years without smiling due to problems after fleeing the war in my country, the Democratic Republic of Congo [DRC]. In the workshop in the refugee camp [Kyangwali] I spent some of the best days in my life. I forgot all about my stressing situation and problems I had as a refugee. I forgot I was a refugee for those days. I was also happy and learned the true power of theatre. (Benson Wereje, Kyangwali Refugee Camp Uganda, August 2010)

In 2008 I was invited to the African Leadership Academy in Johannesburg for a week as a guest artist representing TVO. I had been working on an applied theatre project in Zimbabwe and as Johannesburg, where the academy is based, is not far away, I accepted. The school had only been open a couple of months and its first cohort was in place – selected students from around the continent. The academy seeks '...to transform Africa by developing and supporting future generations of African leaders ... for an innovative two-year programme designed to prepare each student for a lifetime of leadership on the continent' (www.africanleadershipacademy.org).

Students are selected on merit alone. They come from varied backgrounds, from war torn Sudan to Congolese refugees. Each student has shown some kind of outstanding merit, though not necessarily educational. There is the boy from Malawi, William Kamkwamba, who is internationally recognised for his TED (Technology, Entertainment, Design) talks and the novel documenting his life, *The Boy Who Harnessed the Wind: Creating Currents of Electricity and Hope* (2009). There are many children who took on teaching roles in their communities, such as the Ethiopian boy who proposed how the Addis Ababa transport system might be restructured, and the Zimbabwean girl who set up a literacy programme for underprivileged children. The impressive list of students goes on. That this is an exceptional school filled with exceptional individuals is unquestionable. However, it was not the school or these remarkable students that gave me a new belief in Africa's future. It was one boy and the chain of events that began the day I met him.

Joseph Munyambanza was eighteen years old – or so he estimated, as he has no register of his birth so could only guess the year and choose a date for his birth that he liked. This Congolese boy had lived most of his life in a refugee camp in Uganda. At the academy they told me he rarely spoke and he never talked of his life. He would often spend time alone and miss meals. They worried for his welfare and questioned how well he was adjusting to his new scholastic life.

My first job was to talk to the whole school about what I do, applied theatre, and the charity I work with, and then answer their questions. For the week that followed I was to run a series of applied theatre workshops with a group of students, where their personal backgrounds and issues could begin to be dealt with indirectly. At the end of the first day's workshop Joseph, the boy who rarely spoke, sought me out and asked if he could arrange a time to speak with me. I was surprised but pleased and arranged to meet with him the next day.

When Joseph turned up the next afternoon he was extremely polite and a little nervous. He sat down and kept his eyes fixed on the floor. When I asked him what he wanted to speak to me about, he looked up and began to talk. He was focused and confident, but his first language was not English and his speech was laboured as he worked hard to make himself understood and not make mistakes. He spoke non-stop for an hour, telling me about his life and the events that led to his selection for the African Leadership Academy, and about his hopes for the future.

Joseph's story was powerful and heartrending, told in a way that provoked neither pity nor sorrow. He spoke of the bad and the difficult as part of his life story. He was not looking to shock or be pitied. I was amazed by all he had told me and intrigued as to why he had chosen to share so much. This boy clearly did not need therapy. It was equally clear that the school had no reason to fear for his welfare, since Joseph was one of the most level-headed, sharp and aware people I had ever met, with remarkable, constant, unrelenting strength. He was also, I had quickly realised, a boy with a purpose. So I asked him why he was telling me this story.

Joseph smiled and replied, 'Because I want you and your charity to go and do these workshops in the refugee camp.' I had worked on various applied theatre projects in various countries in Africa such as Zimbabwe, South Africa, Tanzania and Kenya and had been asked for money, proposed to, and had children offer themselves for adoption and beg me to take them to my country. But Joseph's request caught me off guard. My brain rapidly tried to process what this would mean – going to stay in a refugee camp. Who would be willing to come with me? How would we survive? How would we get the money to make this happen? And what kind of applied theatre work could I possibly do that would be useful in that situation?

As all this ran through my head. I realised that I could not make such a promise and explained this to Joseph. I told him I would go back and do all I could to find out more about whether or not it was a possibility but that I never made promises unless I knew I could keep them and that this was not a promise I could make. Joseph nodded his head slowly and then asked 'So will you promise?' I smiled, aware that Joseph was not working in his first language and had obviously misunderstood me. I explained again and once again Joseph nodded his head and said 'I understand. Will you promise?' I tried to explain yet again that I only promise if I know absolutely I can do something. 'I understand' he replied and smiled, 'So will you promise?' To Joseph it was simple.

And so I promised. And a few months later, the result of monumental fund-raising and support for the charity, I and two other TVO facilitators packed our bags and headed to the Kyangwali refugee camp for one month. We didn't know what we would find, or even exactly what we would do, but I was determined to fulfil my promise. The team consisted of myself and two facilitators, experienced in areas that I believed would be complementary. Jason is a youth worker specialising in dealing with difficult and challenging young people and a hip-hop artist, freestyler and theatre practitioner. James is a photographer who has worked with TVO over several years, sensitively documenting the work we do. We planned to divide the days into applied theatre sessions which I would lead (men in the morning and women in the afternoon) supported by the others, and then break into groups for song writing and music sessions with the young people based on applied theatre principles, led by Jason and supported by James, while I worked with the women. It had been made clear to us that the men and women would not attend the same workshop.

On reaching Kyangwali we soon saw how difficult life was for the 26,000 or so refugees living there. Disease was rife, people died of malaria daily; water was in poor supply and undrinkable; meningitis was a problem among the children; many refugees suffered from HIV/AIDS and had no medication; food was scarce. How could an applied theatre project hold any value in a place like this? Surely, I thought, these people had far greater needs and would see theatre as a waste of their time and energy.

Next morning we began our workshops. We planned to spend half the day with representatives from the villages within the camp, all of them men, teaching leadership and community skills and ways to deal with the problems in the camp on a community level. Then in the afternoons, I would work with the girls and women in workshops looking at their role in society and the trauma many had been subjected to and witnessed as they fled the DRC. Jason would work with young adults on how to use music and song. Our plan was to teach groups empowerment techniques they could implement after we left. In the music workshops, the youth would learn hip-hop and free-styling and work on how to combine them with their own cultural means of expression. They were to be taught how to compose songs with strong meaning that could encourage and give hope to people in the camp.

We entered Kyangwali with a plan for the workshops already devised. We had researched the camp and the problems within it and arrived with some understanding of the issues we would be tackling, but we found we had made naïve assumptions about the community. What we classified as the hardships or problems needing attention were not the ones the participants believed to be the issues. We were forced to acknowledge that it was not our place to speak for the community and that to do so would be simplistic and dangerous, vulnerable to misrepresentation. Although based on a lot of research, our assumptions meant we would be imposing topics on these people, unintentionally implying they could not speak for themselves. Our work needed to focus on helping participants find their own voice, not speak for them – which inevitably disempowers and alienates.

We learned that we needed to adapt our proposed programme around not only the difficulties of life in the camp but also the inadequacy of our own concepts of what issues needed to be addressed. Applied theatre work requires discussion and negotiation from the outset to ensure that the project belongs to the participants and is not a one-way process. Everyone arrived late on our first day, some by as much as three hours, causing us much frustration at the disjointedness that blocked our attempts to progress with the workshop. I promptly asked Joseph to speak to the group about their punctuality. I have worked on enough projects in Africa to know that African time moves differently, but this was unacceptable. Joseph looked uncomfortable and said that regrettably he would not speak to them. Surprised by his response, I asked him why not. He explained that some of the group were walking for hours each day, some up to four or five hours, to get to the workshops and back home. Others swam a river each day and many who were fully attentive and hard working in the workshops were actually suffering from malaria. If we took account of all this it would be disrespectful to complain about their poor time keeping, he said. I never complained about the time-keeping again.

At the same time, I knew I had to address the timekeeping issue if the workshops were to advance with the least possible disruption. I also knew that with time they would come to love the games, so I scheduled a game session at the start of each day so as to motivate the participants to arrive on time. Another game session was scheduled for the end of the day, an incentive to work hard on all the exercises in the knowledge that they would get to play at the end. The groups loved playing and the games were viewed almost as a treat. In the first week we led the games, but thereafter we asked the participants to lead them. We would often play along but the idea was to let them become accustomed to their own style of play and own way of developing the games. As time went on, the lateness diminished as participants didn't wish to miss a game or exercise. After three years of working there, few ever arrive late. This came about through the refugees implementing a set of rules and processes to ensure timeliness themselves. We never enforced it.

There was so much disunity within the camp itself, so much tension, that I could see that people needed first to learn to play, and only then to learn how games could become a teaching tool. Many had not played for years, and some had never played at all, the war which started when they were infants having robbed them of their childhood. We played games extensively to break up the exercises. I realised that we could use the games to explore basic problems in the camp. For example, in times of sickness it was considered acceptable to carry a woman or a child to a clinic but not a man. For a man to allow himself to be carried was considered shameful. However in cases of malaria and other illnesses this meant that some people could not access the help they needed.

I decided on a range of games that all required physically supporting one another in the group work, such as Minimum Surface Contact, Drop Dead and trust based exercises. Drop Dead proved particularly poignant for them in light of the prevalent malaria. In this game, the group are divided into smaller groups of five and each person has a number from one to five. They all move around the space, mingling with the other groups until a number is called. Whoever has that number must drop dead – unless his teammates can reach him and catch him before he hits the ground. They are not allowed to help anyone who is not in their team. More often than not they will not make it in time to save one another, but as the game proceeds they improve and learn to trust one another more.

I made the exercises progressively harder. They had to calculate how best to bear one another's weight and support their team member to complete the game. After each game I asked what they felt they had learned from it. I didn't tell them what they were intended to learn but allowed them to draw their own conclusions in their own time. This did not always produce the hoped for results. The men saw it as a test of strength to shoulder one another's weight and remarked on this. The village leaders suggested that if they implemented such a system they could help to take sick people, be they male or female, to the clinics – it was their own idea, their realisation and suggestion, nudged along through the game playing.

Another time when disharmony among the group was creating problems, I opted for a game that would unite them by emphasising the need to work together. I blew up balloons and told the group to use them between each person to join themselves in a line. I explained that the balloons represented the people of my village and so they had to take care of every one. Any balloon that burst signified a death in my village. I set them a number of tasks which had to be completed while they balanced the balloons that joined the group together. By the end of the day the twenty balloons were reduced to three and a half! The half balloon had not burst but was slowly losing air. We sat in a circle and looked at the sorry state of my village. I asked what they saw and they explained that sixteen must have died from illness, one clearly had malaria and only three were healthy. I asked what they had learned from the exercise and they sat in silence eyes downcast. Suddenly one of the men slowly raised his hand, 'Since that was your village I think we've learned why there are no white people in the refugee camp!'

At the start of the sessions we spoke to the groups about the issues they felt affected them most. What came up repeatedly was their sense of having lost their identity, and their hate of the word 'refugee':

> We are refugees. We accept that. But that word 'refugee' carries meaning for others, defines us for others in a way that shows they do not understand that we are also human beings, people with hopes and dreams. People who struggle and try to make a better life for ourselves, even when we are given no opportunity to do so. (Emanuel, 2009 Kyangwali refugee camp)

They acknowledged that there were many problems in the camp – HIV/AIDS, rape, corruption and family violence – but identified them as being symptoms of other things. They talked of the alcohol problem rife in the camp and how that caused many of the other issues, yet insisted that alcohol was about trying to erase memories of the war and of the life they had lost, as well knowing they had no future to look forward to. They described how external bodies tried to help by treating these symptoms but ignoring the causes. It became clear that our initial plan would need to be adapted to deal with these over-riding issues, most importantly the loss of identity that being labelled 're-fugee' caused. Workshops would centre on giving voice to the stories of the people in the camp, the stories that had brought them to that place.

When we first entered the camp we caused much consternation with our strange methods. Although the groups participated willingly, they scratched their heads and discussed among themselves how crazy we must be. Despite their doubts, they were open to trying our methods and showed a trust rarely seen in first world societies. Many told us later that they stayed because they had rediscovered laughter through the activities. Even when we worked with serious issues they felt rejuvenated and excited to learn to play as children again or even for the first time. For many this was a serious step and people would gather and watch us at play, some critical that village leaders and pastors were engaging in such frivolity. Later when we asked them why they had stayed in those initial meetings they replied that it was because it was the first time people had come into the camp and asked to hear their voice, their stories.

They explained that many organisations came to the camp to give them seminars on topics such as AIDS prevention, avoiding or treating malaria, education and other topics. They would sit and be spoken to, often in a language they did not understand, or given information leaflets which many could not read. They felt ashamed when told to take notes for most did not own pen or paper, and some had never learned to write. Nobody, they said, had ever come into the camp and asked *them* to speak, listened to *their* stories and problems and then worked with them to find a way to voice such things. Nobody, they said, had ever played with them. They now use their own applied theatre techniques to teach all these things in the camp, giving voice to others and laughing and playing with them in the process.

We now arrive in the camp each year with notebooks and pens, not because we expect the groups to take notes, but because it gives them a sense of importance. I also learned quickly that much weight was given to allowing for discussion time. Whether this was sitting in a circle and talking during the workshop, or allocating a time at the end, it was considered respectful to allow this period of discussion, which could run on for hours. Despite the language barrier, we were expected to sit with them throughout, even if the discussion did not involve us or our work. On one such occasion a pastor spoke about how surprised he had been by our work and by us as people.

> My grandfather told me that white people eat black people, so when you see them you must run. Every day I sat next to Jennifer to see if she would try to bite me but she never did! My grandfather was wrong, Jennifer didn't bite me and she is a human being just like us. We are all the same. Now I will tell the children they must go to school and learn about these things. I am an old man but I am learning. (Pastor Agustin, 2009 Kyangwali refugee camp)

In terms of what we had planned for this first trip, I guess we failed. Applied theatre's strength however, surely lies in its flexibility and ability to adapt to meet the needs and demands of those who are taking part in it. In the years that followed, we adapted our projects in Kyangwali to deal with what the participants feel is most significant for them at that time. The TVO team who travel to the camp changes according to our goals. They are chosen each time on the basis of the skills we are hoping to share with the groups, so while there is some overlap at times, there is an infusion of new blood into the team every year.

It would be easy to look at these developments and imagine a project that flowed smoothly, but this was not the reality. We faced many problems over the years such as illness and inconsistent attendance. From one year to the next we lost people we had trained, sometimes through death, sometimes because they had left the refugee camp to return, despite the dangers, to their country in hopes of a better life.

Time moves slowly in Kyangwali and even the weather can affect the day's attendance and work. Heavy rains can make a pathway impassable within minutes and create mudslides and flooding that destroys homes. We had to avoid imposing our sense of right and wrong on others, as this only alienated them and was disrespectful of their cultural norms. We found this difficult at times since some of their cultural practices seemed to us violent, dangerous and wrong. We constantly reminded ourselves that we are in no position to judge. The voice of the group, and their participation as they develop the work, prevented us from forcing our own views on them and compelled us to ensure the participants lead the project.

When we first started working in Kyangwali we were told about a charity organisation which worked there before us. They held seminars with the men to teach them how to be better husbands and fathers. They told them it was wrong for them to beat their wives and to leave the rearing of their children entirely to the women. Some of the more open-minded men decided to implement these strange practices and the results were devastating. A number of women asked their local pastors to grant a divorce, complaining that their husband was trying to assume their role with the children so was questioning their ability as a mother. Other women complained their husband no longer loved them because they weren't beating them any more. Most cases were resolved, but some did end in divorce and severe criticism was levelled at the men by their communities.

We were dismayed by these accounts. Like so many projects worldwide, the charity had tried to treat symptoms instead of causes. Trying to change a culturally accepted practice can have serious implications and we have to be careful that what we are unravelling does not end up doing more damage. The problem of rape in the camp was one example. Although condemned, it was rarely punished. All too often cases were not only dismissed but actually considered entertaining. For example, if a man was drunk he was not considered responsible for his actions and his alcohol fuelled sexual drive was considered natural and understandable. Searching for ways to deal with these kinds of contradictions, I listened to their stories, watched their sketches and tried to learn from them. Learning more about their attitudes helped me search out ways in to the problem and how to deal with what it was that had created these attitudes in the first place, what lay behind them.

We found it especially difficult to come to terms with the nature of the sketches they created and their reactions to them. We watched sketch after sketch depicting rapes in the camp. To our frustration the audience, especially the women, laughed and cheered, supporting the claims that no man is responsible for his actions when under the influence of alcohol. The refugees did not consider rape to be the issue but believed we should be investigating why so many people in the camp turn to excessive drinking. This brought us back to the negative connotations of the label 'refugee', but also to the situation that had caused them to flee their country and become refugees. Concerned as I was about the rape situation, I had to step back from it and deal with the issues the group felt were more pressing. For them it was simple: had war not ravaged their country and destroyed their lives, leaving them homeless and bereft of their loved ones, they would not have become refugees. Had they not become refugees their lives would not be plagued with poverty, disease and lack of hope for the future and so they would not have turned to drink. And had they not turned to drink, the rapes would not occur. So, they assured me, it was clear that rape was not the problem.

Making assumptions can lead to misguided oversimplifying in our work. I brought up the topic of rape with the women, in an effort to grasp at the community's attitude to it. I was concerned by the practice of blaming the woman, in many cases forcing her to marry the rapist, or expelling her from the village if she could not get her rapist's agreement to marry her. They too created sketch after sketch but these spent too much time depicting the rape and not enough on exploring the consequences. The sketches left the women in fits of laughter, and they said they found many of the situations 'funny'. Afterwards one of the women told me I had to remember that Africans like to be entertained so if you want to change something you must entertain them and make them laugh. That doesn't mean they don't appreciate how serious the issue is, she explained, simply that you have to get their attention in a certain way. The women knew how to go about this and I had to abandon all my first world western upbringing was telling me.

It was difficult to accept that I would have to try to work with the women to create a new approach that allowed for discussion and educating about the problem and ways to prevent it, yet allowed them to be entertaining and funny. I was extremely uncomfortable with this; I would look around at people laughing at what I considered unnecessarily descriptive and graphic rape scenes, baffled by their reactions. Yet this was the approach they felt comfortable with and believed would be effective with audiences. And they were right. The women went on to perform some of the scenes in the camp and the discussions which followed were animated and purposeful. Decisions were made about actions that could be taken to deal with the problem of rape. They devised a war cry that would alert others to what was happening so villagers would know to run to a woman's aid. They established a structure by which women could report a rape. This was quite new – most rapes are never reported. A pairing programme was set up to ensure that no female went alone to collect water, as the walk to the remote water tank put them in danger.

Working with the groups in the Kyangwali refugee camp threw up many cross cultural barriers, but we gradually learned what was acceptable. After two years, we were finally able to combine men and women in the groups. They were at last willing to act together and to play games together. This was a major achievement. It had not come easily to the group, nor been pain free for me. In my first year I had spent a lot of time teaching them about trust games, bringing them to an exercise called Joe Egg, where one member would stand in the middle, eyes closed and allow themselves to fall against the circle and be passed around the group. I explained this in great detail to the men's group and, seeing the doubt and concern on their faces, agreed to be the first person to go in the middle. I crossed my hands in front of my chest, closed my eyes and fell back trustingly, only to smash down on broken concrete as the men parted ways. As I lay there horrified, cut and bruised, they explained that it was not appropriate or respectful for them to touch me in that way. Of course nobody told me this beforehand, and this too, I learned, was part of the cultural difference. When I asked why nobody had thought to mention this important fact, I received the answer I am now so used to hearing, 'You didn't ask!'

Working with translators in a camp that hosts so many nationalities (the refugees come from five different countries, although in recent years most are Congolese) and many local languages (at last count twelve were spoken), we decided to balance our work between English and Swahili to ensure everyone present could understand. Each workshop took twice as long as usual as we worked through selective translations. Our translators would decide whether what we said was worth translating in its entirety, but also whether they agreed with what we said. If they disagreed the translation took on a life of its own and my single sentence could easily take ten minutes to translate and be followed by animated discussion to which I was not privy.

One of my greatest challenges has been working with the women's group in the camp and I still find it difficult. They have certainly progressed but progress has been so slow and so hard-earned that it can be hard to see. On my very first meeting with the women, I gathered them to play some simple games. I put them in a circle and explained that I would call the name of someone in the circle and throw the ball to her. She would then choose some-one and do the same and so on. I and the other facilitators gave examples for clarity. But when I called the first woman's name and threw the ball, she kept her hands firmly by her sides and the ball bounced off her body and rolled away. I tried again with a different woman but got the same result. I tried placing the ball in the hands of one woman and asked her to try. As I stepped back she let the ball fall to the ground. I later learned that their fear of failure and their belief that they were incapable of what I was asking them to do pre-vented them from cooperating. Meanwhile I was left with a group of women who would not even talk to one another, far less to me, and who refused to take part in any game I suggested. They would move into position as an exer-cise was explained and then remain there immobile when the game was meant to begin.

After two days of this I told my co-facilitators at our daily evaluation meeting that every day as the time for the women's workshop drew close, I would pray for rain so it would be cancelled. The truth is I was out of ideas, exhausted and frustrated from getting nowhere with them. The co-facilitators looked horri-fied and said they had never heard me talk like that. I was too disillusioned to feel ashamed of my reaction. I truly wanted it to rain and the thought of three more weeks of these workshops was driving me to despair.

The next day I decided the only way forward was to come clean and tell the women how I felt and ask them how I could progress. When I explained this to the women, they exchanged puzzled looks. I asked them how they felt about this and they replied promptly and eloquently that they had no idea what I was talking about. They explained that they greatly enjoyed the games (despite their lack of participation), that they valued what they were learning and were keen to progress with the workshops. I could not understand what I was hearing. One of the translators came to sit beside me and placed an arm around my shoulders, 'Jennifer, don't you think the problem is with you and your idea of progress and success? It seems you are the only one struggling in this workshop.' I felt I had been punched in the gut. It was true.

A few years on, the group has advanced and some of the women have joined the camp's theatre group, where men and women work together. I still struggle with the group and working with them has often led me to question my suitability as a facilitator. I feel frustrated and at the same time guilty about my impatience. Yet they have opened up, they have become adept at many of the games and they create clever and informative sketches. Progress has been slow and laboured every step of the way. And despite the frequent long silences and expressionless faces, the women speak of their joy at being in the group. Learning not to judge success by my own understanding of what that is has been difficult and will probably continue to be so.

Today the inhabitants of Kyangwali have their own applied theatre group called *Ibyiringiro Bisha* (New Hope), run by and for refugees. They conduct their own versions of applied theatre workshops across Kyangwali and neighbouring camps. Two members have returned to the DRC and initiated a similar group there, teaching what they have learned and exploring new ways to use applied theatre in war-torn Eastern Congo.

Over the years we have taught *Ibyiringiro Bisha* various techniques and then watched as they butchered them into a form they thought more appropriate. Yet by doing so they found a way to speak directly to their communities, that made sense and appealed to them. I always teach that in this work you must first learn the rules in order to break them. And so I stood back and watched as they broke almost every rule I had ever taught. In the process they discovered their own method and approach that outstripped any I could have taught them. They adapted the work according to the cultural awareness and sensitivity that came from living the issues they were dealing with in their theatre work.

We worked with physical theatre and explored how to combine movement into meaningful dance to teach about their lives. Afterwards we watched their performance in which they used the technique to explain about malaria. I expected it to be about what to do to prevent it, but it was about what happened to your body when malaria took over. The dance expressed the pain, vomiting, coughing and spitting and the culmination in death. We were shocked by the graphic visual and audible displays but our doubts were soon silenced by the community discussions that sprang up afterwards about how to prevent malaria and use mosquito nets properly. The group understand how to appeal to the community, what entertains them and makes them laugh, and succeeds in getting the message across. Every year TVO has taught new skills to *Ibyiringiro Bisha* and shown them how these can be used in an applied theatre approach. To date, they have learned about forum theatre, image theatre, improvisation, physical theatre, puppetry, freestyling, hip hop and clowning. Enabling them to form their own identity and grow, often through trial and error, has required us to let go as facilitators.

Joseph Munyambanza continues to work with us in Kyangwali when he can (he is currently studying a pre-medicine college course in the USA) and to challenge those who try to label him. This was clear in his graduation speech from the African Leadership Academy in June 2010, entitled *More than a Label* (see appendix) where he talked about what it means to be a refugee in the eyes of others.

TVO continues to work in Kyangwali and to look for new ways to help the community in addition to supporting the theatre group *Ibyiringiro Bisha*. In 2009 we raised funds to build a primary school and initiated an educational programme called Right to Learn which sponsors orphans to receive good education, food and care. We support a project for girls and young women called Anti-Violence which offers a safe house for women and girls in trouble, counselling and the opportunity to learn skills such as tailoring. The projects continue to grow and *Ibyiringiro Bisha* now trains others in neighbouring camps and on the DRC border, helping them plan similar work.

Principles and practice
- The safety of the facilitating team should always be a priority
- Egos need to be kept in check. Remember that the project is about the group, not about the facilitating team
- Everyone involved in an applied theatre project is both student and teacher, both participant and facilitator
- Use the knowledge of the groups you are working with and show how the methods can be applied to their knowledge base and experience
- Working with translators can be challenging and the additional time and comprehension issues must be factored into the project
- Take care with cultural assumptions and research carefully
- Always follow up exercises with a discussion period, no matter how brief, to enable processing
- Many of the exercises from Theatre of the Oppressed and other practices must be adapted to meet cultural needs and restrictions
- There must be a flexibility and ability to adapt to the individual needs and demands of each group

- Approaching a negative issue from a positive angle will better encourage discussion and participation
- Working with different cultures and in different countries, we must take care not to judge the work produced (or the reaction to it) by our own cultural standards
- Avoid enforcing your own approach or way of thinking
- What we might classify as the hardships or problems needing attention will not necessarily be those the participants identify and it is they who should always have the final say
- Emphasise that there is no right or wrong way to do things in the workshops, encouraging an attitude of exploration
- Proposing changes to a culturally accepted practice can have serious implications and care must be taken to ensure that we don't do more damage with our work

Conclusion

Augusto Boal said the Theatre of the Oppressed (TO) stimulated a transformation in people. His practice was based on identifying oppression and basing his techniques of breaking that oppression on specific incidents and people. In other words people were being told that their state of oppression was wrong and they needed to change it. For me, identifying a state of oppression is about allowing it to exist. Transformation is not necessarily what someone is seeking and it might not be productive at that point in their lives.

For Boal empowerment came through action; for me it comes through understanding. I believe people should be allowed to be where they are, at any given time, and not feel that this is wrong and that they have to transform themselves and their situation. I hope to explore their situation with them through my work, gain a deeper understanding of all the factors involved and guide them towards a clearer understanding of their behaviour and their perceptions of others. If they decide to pursue change, that will be their decision and their journey. The workshops serve as a support, even a guide on that journey, but it remains a personal and individual undertaking.

Our society is constantly telling us what we should and should not do, how we should behave and think. I have worked with people who have been victims of abuse, who feel shame at being classified as victims and are troubled more by that label than by what is happening to them. They are told they must act to change their situation. But do we have the right to tell anyone to change their situation? And does this help in the long run? They need first to understand their situation and might decide that they do not want to change it. Telling people to change can lead to a repetition of the problem if it occurs without any understanding of the transformation. Telling refugees, for example, to transform their situation is unlikely to be productive in a place where they have few alternatives. Together we can explore their situation, gain new understandings and hopefully I can help give a voice to people who have been silenced.

Boal appeared to be trying to fix people, and this assumes that they are broken. But in whose opinion? I prefer to see people as travellers on a journey with many possible paths. There can be no judgement along the way. Whether working with prison inmates, torturers, gangs or victims, there can be no exploration if there is judgment. The journey begins with an acceptance of the now.

Although influenced by TO, my work is not limited to it or by it. I saw how effective TO could be, how experimentation with and adaption of Boal's methods could work with any group, regardless of age, culture or background. But there is no denying that TO can be problematic. It is frequently misunderstood, mistaught and misapplied, and can cause more harm than good as a result. No theory should stand still and in theatre no methodology can afford to. The use of TO, especially in the applied theatre arena, requires constant development and study. I myself use it as a progressive set of ideas to be adapted and refined with each project.

Over the years of working in applied theatre I have had to learn to read intuitively what is happening around me. I work through a process of observation and reflection, trial and error. Every project becomes a learning experience to sharpen those skills for the next one. We have learned not to assume that all people work in the same way, that they all see the same things we do – and that has presented me with challenges of my own. Writing this book helped me remember that everyone sees things differently and I have had to step back time and again and try to explain processes I took for granted.

Every project reads like a map in our head. We must see the connecting paths and move between them constantly, finding a way around the obstacles. I was reminded of these things in a recent workshop. I was tired and distracted and, as I watched the group, I realised that my brain was not processing as it would normally. I felt uncertain what the next step should be and, as a result, felt tied to the pre-prepared plan regardless of whether or not it was working well. I panicked momentarily, but at the same time felt bemused by my own reaction and inability to see alternatives. I had to think about how I normally work, and the intuitive processes I have frequently taken so for granted. Stepping back from the situation allowed me to piece together the puzzle, to create the map with all its connecting paths in my head. I know every piece in the workshop connects and I have to be sufficiently removed from it to see those patterns and trust the methods that will get me there.

It is crucial to remember that everything connects. There are no random games or exercises – everything that is done creates a new connection and then another and another. A word that is said creates a link to another exercise and shows us when we need to change direction. So we must always be listening to the participants, who will guide the direction based on their needs and desires in the exploration process. But everything that is done is and must be connected. If we reject an exercise it must be because we have sensed a change in the group and we have a better one to replace it with; if we switch direction in the middle of a workshop it is because we have seen how to advance better in another way. It is not because we don't like the results or the reactions, as a group complains or blocks where we are heading. It is about seeing what is needed, even when the group are unable to and always having a well prepared plan to ground us. It is this same plan that enables us to have a bank of alternative exercises to help us change direction if necessary. This can only be developed from experience and a willingness and openness to the experimental nature of applied theatre work.

We have found that teamwork is crucial to every project, offering support, sharing and guidance. An ideal team has a range of expertise and the members are constantly learning from one another and developing as a result. At times I have been the only facilitator because of circumstances outside of my control. In these instances I have set up a team network to check in with, discuss progress, brainstorm ideas and share concerns. Support is essential, as is the range of perspectives gained.

Over the years I have been privileged to work in so many varied projects, exploring the work of applied theatre and honing my own techniques and style. At times the work has been exhilarating and challenging, at others I have felt bruised and drained. I have learned from each experience and from the people I have worked with. Part of the growing process as a practitioner is to learn to be kind to yourself. When you make mistakes, when you see you could have used a better approach, when responses have been unpredictable, it is necessary to treat it as part of the learning process and not beat yourself up for not having done things better. This can be achieved by distance and by the support of a team. Ultimately it is about applying the processes we work with to ourselves, understanding the role of perception we are subject to, and the importance of self reflection as practitioners, allowing ourselves to be where we are at each stage in our own learning process .

What I can say with certainty is that the work is never dull. While it is challenging I've always had fun, whether through the games, the exercises, or simply the opportunity to work with the various groups. I have met incredible people and been inspired by working with them. They have taught me so much about my practice and myself as a person, so helping my knowledge in this field to expand. Applied theatre is a developing field of work which places demands upon us mentally, physically and emotionally. The work can be frustrating, depleting, exciting, unpredictable and rewarding. But it is without doubt always challenging, meaningful and filled with purpose.

After over a decade of adventures, a few bruises and close encounters, I look forward to what the next years have in store.

Epilogue
More than a Label

Speech given by Joseph Munyambanza at the African Leadership Academy Inaugural class graduation, 5th June 2010

I am Joseph Munyambanza. My home country is the Democratic Republic of Congo but I have lived most of my life in Kyangwali refugee camp in Uganda.

When I was 6 years old, war came to my village. We were forced to run or we would be shot or taken to be child soldiers. We ran and when we stopped running we had no home anymore and many of us had no family.

And so when I was 6 years old I became a refugee.

I learned that being a refugee meant that I was 'nobody'. I had no rights. I had no identity. I was expected to fail in life. I would have little or no education. I should expect nothing from the future. I probably would not survive. If starvation and malaria did not kill us, anger, hatred and lack of hope would.

This was not the life I had imagined for myself. I had hopes and dreams like other children. But now I was just a refugee. I thought I had rights, an identity, but they called me a refugee and took that away from me. They said it was their right to do so.

When I was 7 years old I realised that to change my life I needed an education. I needed to have hope and I needed to believe in the future. And so at 7 years old I began a journey; that journey would bring me to the African Leadership Academy almost ten years later.

In the camp I went to school every day and I studied hard. It was not easy. In the morning I would get up very early and dig. My hands were covered in blisters and bleeding. Then I would go to school. Often I was hungry, we had little food, sometimes we had no food – until I came [to the Academy] I never knew what it was like to have a full stomach. I was tired and I would try to study late at night with a candle when my parents were asleep. Life was not easy but I was one of the lucky ones. School brought me happiness and motivation. School gave me hope.

There were sad moments in my life, but I was determined to be strong, determined to help myself and other people in the camp to have a better life and show the world that we are not disposable just because we are refugees. I became even more determined when I lost my older sister. She died in pregnancy – the nurses refused to help her because she had no money. We are refugees but we are people and we deserve to be treated with humanity not to be dismissed and left to die because we are poor. I decided I would work hard on my education and become a doctor, not to escape the refugee camp, but so I could return and help people ... people like my sister.

As I became a teenager I met some other boys who thought like me and together we formed a club called COBURWAS. We had a vision. The name represents different countries, as we had refugees from Congo, Burundi, Uganda, Rwanda and Sudan. Our aim is to work not only in refugee camps, for we understand that most Africans have problems, not just refugees. We found out that the best way to create change was to bring the youth together. There were many challenges to address, and education was the most important. We did not have money to pay children's' school fees but we encouraged those who had dropped out of school to go back, and we raised money by digging for people during the day. We decided to buy textbooks, which could help many children at once, and began tutoring programmes. Students in the camp did not have quality education and so we revise with them and created a mentoring programme. Grades began to improve and more children were attending school.

By the time I was 17 years old, just three years later, we had opened two hostels in a neighbouring town to enable students to go to high school and have a place to stay. Sometimes we have no food, we struggle to get the money for fees and rent, many have become ill with malaria and some of our friends have died, but we all share a vision and work relentlessly to achieve it.

We also opened a COBURWAS school in the refugee camp where the children could get quality education. The school continues to grow. We started club activities for the children, playing soccer and other things so that they can do exercise and have fun like children who are not refugees.

We are always seeking ways to be more self-sustaining, to not always depend on help from others. We have a cooperative with a small farm and even a small restaurant now. We are teaching dressmaking so that we can make goods and sell them.

In all this time I was often troubled by the bad situation for the girls and women in the camp. Many have been raped, many are forced to marry at a young age and they are denied an education. I knew this had to change and so I began a club we called Anti-violence, to give support to our girls and women. Here they can have meetings, counselling, support for their education and learn dressmaking and other skills.

On 25th August 2008 I left the camp and all those people whom I love, and came to join a second family here at the African Leadership Academy thanks to the support of Eric Glustorm and Educate. In my first year here a guest speaker came to the school, Dr Jennifer Hartley, and she did workshops about her work empowering people and working with difficult situations. I approached her and told her my story and asked if she and her charity, Theatre versus Oppression, could help us in the refugee camp. Just a few months later the refugee camp joined with Jennifer's charity and with money they raised we began to build a school which will be the foundation for our future.

I am sure the suffering in the refugee camp and other places is not that people are helpless, but because at times they have no one to show them a beginning. It is not easy no matter how wise you may be to get the exact direction or route without anyone to guide you. Communities are like eggs. Even though the egg may be fertilised, if it is not hatched or incubated, it can never produce a chick.

I have had many people to guide me in my life and many are here today, including Eric and Jennifer who came to see me graduate. Many others are with me in spirit to celebrate this special day. In the last two years I have worked hard to be a better student and a better person. It is my dream now to go to university and study to be a doctor. It is a difficult dream but my life has often been difficult and I will never give up hope.

In my life I have had to ask for many things – for food to survive, for help to get an education, for belief in my plans and ideas. I have asked many things but I have never lost my pride. I am Joseph Munyambanza. My home country is the Democratic Republic of Congo. They call me a refugee.

I am a man.
I am African.
I am a student and a teacher.
I am a brother and a son.

I am a friend.
I am a leader.
I am a dreamer and a realist.
I am many things.
I am so much more than the label 'refugee'.
I am Joseph Munyambanza.

Thank you.

References

Blatner, A (2007) *Interactive and Impovisational Drama: Varieties of applied theatre and performance.* New York: iUniverse, Inc.

Boal, A (1979) *Theatre of the Oppressed.* New York: Urizen

Boal, A (1995) *Rainbow of Desire.* London: Routledge

Boal, A (2001) *Hamlet and the Baker's Son: My life in theatre and politics.* London: Routledge

Boal, A (2002) 2nd ed. *Games for Actors and Non-Actors.* New York: Routledge

Freire, P (2000) *Pedagogy of the Oppressed (30th Anniversary Edition).* New York: Continuum

Freire, P (2000) *Pedagogy of Freedom: Ethics, Democracy and Civic Courage.* London: Rowman and Littlefield.

Hartley, JS (2005) *The Art of Silence.* Asunción: Arandura Editorial

Hartley, JS (2007) *The Sin Eater.* Asunción: Arandura Editorial

hooks, b (1994) *Teaching to Transgress. Education as the practice of freedom.* London: Routledge

Jackson, A (2007) *Theatre, Education and the Making of Meanings: Art or Instrument?* Manchester University Press

Jones, P (1996) *Drama as Therapy – Theatre as Living.* London: Routledge

Kamkwamba, W and Mealer, B (2009) *The boy who harnessed the wind: Creating currents of electricity and hope.* HarperTrue: New York

Landy, RJ (1986) *Drama Therapy: Concepts and Practices.* Springfield: Charles C. Thomas

Landy, RJ (1993) *Persona and Performance: The meaning of role in drama, therapy, and everyday life.* New York: The Guilford Press

Nicholson, H (2005) *Applied Drama (Theatre and Performance Practices).* New York: Palgrave Macmillan

Robinson, K (2001) *Out of Our Minds; Learning to be Creative.* Chichester: Capstone Publishing Limited

Rodd, M (1998) *Theatre for Community, Conflict and Dialogue: The Hope is Vital Training Manual.* Portsmouth: Heinemann

Taylor, P (2003) *Applied Theatre: Creating Transformative Encounters in the Community.* Portsmouth: Heinemann

Thompson, J (2003) *Applied Theatre: Bewilderment and beyond (Stage and screen studies).* Peter Lang Publishing Inc

Thompson, J (2005) *Digging Up Stories: Applied Theatre, Performance and War.* Manchester University Press

Prendergast, M and Saxton, J (2009) *Applied Theatre: International Case Studies and Challenges for Practice.* Bristol: Intellect Books

Prentki, T and Preston, S (2009) *Applied Theatre Reader.* London: Routledge

Wa Wamwere, K (2003) *Negative ethnicity: from bias to genocide.* Seven Stories Press

Interviews

Barreto, E (25 August 2004) Interviewed by JS Hartley in Asunción, Paraguay

Barreto, E (13 April 2005) Interviewed by JS Hartley in Asunción, Paraguay

Boal, A (3 June 2005) Interview by J Gonzalez www.democracynow.org/2005/6/3/famed_brazilian_artist_augusto_boal_on (Accessed January 2011)

Munyambanza, J (27 October 2008) Interviewed by JS Hartley in Johannesburg, South Africa

Wereje, B (6 August 2010) Interviewed by JS Hartley in Kyangwali Refugee Camp, Uganda

Websites

African Leadership Academy website available at <http:www.africanleadershipacademy.org> (Accessed 12 December 2011)

Munyambanza, J., Graduation speech for the African Leadership Academy in Johannesburg, South Africa on 5 June 2010.

Part 1 <http://www.youtube.com/watch?v=EN8vm5FqrOl&feature=related>

Part 2 <http://www.youtube.com/watch?v=8X7_S-Fi41A> (Accessed on 13 December 2010)

TEDx talk by JS Hartley entitled *The Truth in the Lie* available at <http://www.youtube.com/watch?v=vF5an8JHrOQ> (Accessed January 2012)

Theatre versus Oppression website available at: <http://www.theatreversusoppression.com> (Accessed February 2012)

Appendix
Glossary of games and exercises

The games and exercises listed below are from a variety of sources. Some are from Augusto Boal's Theatre of the Oppressed work (AB), some are adaptations of games for which the original source cannot be traced (source unknown SU) but that are commonly used within drama settings, some are from an unknown source but adapted by me (SU adapted by JH) and some have been created by me over the years (JH).

Agora Mode (AB 1995:64)

Used with a prepared scene or a forum presentation. The protagonist is removed from the scene, the remaining actors discuss the situation and the protagonist remains in character throughout the discussion. New information may be revealed, conflict built, allies created and so on. The exercise is repeated for each character in the scene, allowing the different perspectives on what is happening to develop.

Angel/Devil (JH)

In character the actor speaks a monologue from a play, sketch or her thoughts. Seated behind her on either side are the angel and devil inside her and they whisper her thoughts and intentions from their perspective. They have no physical contact with the actor in the middle and must stay in their seats, so they must look for ways to make themselves heard. The actor tries to focus on her monologue and not be distracted by what she is hearing. Discussion with the whole group afterwards looks at what has happened and the changes which have occurred.

Variations

- the angel and devil are allowed to move around and have agreed upon contact with the actor in the middle
- rather than a monologue the actor in the middle simply explains her situation and then engages with the angel and devil as each tries to win her over to their way of thinking

- after some time the actor in the middle is removed and the angel and devil are left to argue out the situation between themselves

- the interaction between the angel and devil is changed – first one seated and the other standing but no physical contact; then reverse this; next both standing but no physical contact; finally allowing physical contact

- angel and devil are removed and the actor in character repeats her monologue, or speaks about her current frame of mind as a result of what he has heard

The Bigger Story (JH)

Based on working from a play, sketch or a specific problem that has been discussed beforehand. Whole group forms a large circle and everyone takes on a role associated with the characters, such as son, daughter, grandfather, employer and so on. Every group is different, choosing characters according to their own perceptions of the situation and so it is important the participants volunteer for these roles. Once all the characters have been decided, two are chosen to go into the middle of the circle and strike up a conversation in character. After a few minutes, one is removed and a new person enters. This means characters who would not normally cross paths suddenly find themselves in the centre, forced to conduct a conversation with an unlikely counterpart. Each time a new conversation begins the circle must respect any information revealed and can build on it if relevant. There are no changes to who is in the centre unless called by the facilitator; no physical contact at any time and the two in the centre must remain there for the allocated time even if they choose not to speak. At times the story will take a new direction, a new main character might develop, or a new issue, underlying the one originally being dealt with.

As the group becomes more experienced, settings other than the circle can be chosen and characters are moved in and out of the various settings to hold the conversations (eg. with prison work the setting could include a prison cell, a court room, the house and the pub). Reactions and conversations that develop are then influenced also by the locations (this variation does require greater acting skill and so it is wiser to move into it only when participants are comfortable with the concept).

Example: To get participants accustomed to the exercise I often begin with a fairytale, asking them to recap a favourite fairytale and then allocate all the roles by asking what other characters are implied by the story. One group elected to do *Little Red Riding Hood*. The characters cast were Red, the grandmother, the wolf, the huntsman and the mother. Other implied characters included the grandfather, the wolf's parents, Red's father and elder sister. As the conversations developed in the centre the story took on a new slant. Like most fairytales, the story was about dysfunctional families. The grandfather had left the grandmother but was secretly living in the basement of the house. He wanted to divorce the grandmother but their prenuptial agreement meant he would lose the house and all her money. He had hired the wolf to kill the grandmother so he could return and lay claim to the money and property.

Change! (SU adapted by JH)

The group are seated on chairs in a circle while one person standing in the middle shouts CHANGE. Everyone must change their seat and the person in the middle tries to get a seat, leaving a new person stuck in the middle. Participants must change to a new seat each time and cannot take one on either side of them. After this warm up, the person in the middle completes a sentence which begins 'I think/ believe/feel/regret...' with a statement about themselves. Anyone who agrees with the statement must change chairs, while the person who made the statement will try to sit on one of the freed up seats.

Drop Dead (adaption by JH of Fainting at Frejus AB 2002:158)

The class are divided into groups of 4 or 5 and each person in the group takes a number from 1-5. The groups move around the room in all directions but do not walk alongside others in their own group. The facilitator calls a number and people with that number must immediately drop dead. It is the responsibility of the others in their specific group to try to catch them before they fall. More than one number can be called at a time.

Feedback summaries (SU adapted by JH)

These simple exercises can be carried out at the start or end of a session:

- participants shape their bodies into an image to represent what they are feeling about the workshop at the moment
- participants form groups and, in silence, create images of how they feel they are progressing or feelings they have about the project or topic being dealt with
- in a circle each participant shares how they are feeling in a single word. This is very difficult but it usually ensures that the word is carefully selected
- a combination of the above. Participants make an image and when all are complete they choose a word to match their image
- instead of a word the participants share what their Facebook status would be in that moment with regard to the workshop
- participants are asked to work in groups to explore what they feel they are struggling with in the workshop. Each person in the group takes a turn to make their sculpted image, which should not include themselves. Each group discusses their thoughts and feelings about the images, what was similar or distinct, or what felt familiar. Each group creates one composite image from all those presented and

finally the entire group makes one composite image from all of these, moving from the individual to the collective and working through what they all find recognisable in one another's struggle

Fighting Cocks (AB 2002:170, adapted by JH)

The group are divided into pairs. One person accuses the other of something and they must try to defend and justify themselves. It must never be stated what the person is being accused of and so the argument must gain and sustain momentum without this ever being known.

Human Knot (SU)

Participants form a circle, shoulder-to-shoulder. Each places one hand in the middle of the circle to grasp another person's hand, then puts their other hand in the middle, ensuring they grasp a different person's hand. Without letting go of the hands they are clasping, they must now untangle themselves to create a circle.

Variations

- ▨ group forms a circle, holding hands, maintaining contact during the whole exercise, then one person begins to move, and others follow, going over and under hands and arms, until no one can move. Then without breaking the hand contact, the group attempts to unknot itself
- ▨ the same exercise with eyes closed (in a line or n a tight circle), join hands with two people opposite then try to untie

Me myself and I (JH)

Working silently in groups of three, one person moulds the other two to represent two contrasting views of himself; how he views himself and how he believes he is viewed by others. He does not tell the statues which version of himself they represent. When the sculptor is happy with his work, he approaches each statue and speaks to them, providing them with three words he feels describes each and then moves to stand behind the two statues. The statues are now armed with two pieces of information: the shape they have been moulded into and the three words allocated them. They now come to life to create a monologue about who they are, although they remain unable to move their bodies. This continues for approximately five minutes. When the monologue section is complete, the sculptor stands with his back to the statues so that all three have their backs to one another. He places himself in a position representative of how he desires to be and be seen. There are now three statues: how the sculptor views himself, how he believes others see him, and his 'ideal'. The sculptor proceeds, still with his back to the other two statues, to describe the changes he would need to make to himself and in his life to achieve his ideal. If convinced by what they hear, each statue moves a little to represent how that change would affect their position. When the sculptor finishes speaking, the three statues turn to face one another and compare their similarities and differences through discussion.

Memory Game (SU adapted by JH)

Used when a group share a similar story or have all been part of the same incident/ experience. The group sit in a circle while one person sits in the storyteller's chair and tells their story. If any of the others listening thinks the storyteller has omitted any detail, they stop them, change places and continue with their own version until another makes a similar challenge and so on.

Variation: begin with the end of the story following the same procedure.

Minimum Surface Contact (AB 2002:56-57, adapted by JH)

The class is divided into groups. The facilitator calls out a total number of body parts, eg. 2 hands and 2 feet. Each individual group must discuss and find a way to combine their bodies as one unit, so that only the allowed body parts are touching the floor and everything else is raised off the ground without using the support of walls, chairs, tables etc.

Paper Chase (SU adapted by JH)

The group divide into pairs, each holding a sheet of paper between their foreheads. The paper must be connected between the two bodies at all times. Without using their hands they must try to move the paper down their bodies until it is between their ankles, and then return it back up until it is between their foreheads again. If the paper falls it must be returned to where it was before it fell.

Variation: group stand in a line with each person connected to another only by a sheet of paper between them. No hands are allowed and the group must try to manoeuvre its way around the space with the paper falling.

Rashomon (AB 2002:236, 1995:115-116)

Used with a prepared scene or a forum presentation. The protagonist makes an exaggerated image, involving the whole body, of how they felt and saw each of the other characters during the preceding scene. These images are referred to as masks. The masks are taken on by each character. The protagonist makes a final mask, an image of how they felt and saw themself. Keeping their images as masks, the characters then try to repeat the scene. The masks may make movement and speech difficult but the actors must stay with their mask regardless. Each of the other characters then creates a set of masks from their perspectives and the scene is repeated, with the number of improvisations each time depending on the number of characters. When all the images have been generated from each character's perspective, the scene is improvised once more but now the characters can alternate between the masks they have worn and choose the one that feels most comfortable to them or that best helps them to obtain what they want.

Same and Different (SU)

This can be used within a group activity to emphasise similar experiences by acknowledging the differences that exist in their personal experiences. The group sits in a semi-circle, with one person in the middle. The person in the middle tells the story of his experience for about one minute. The listeners note down three points that are similar to their own experience and three points that are different. After one minute a new person moves to the middle and begins to tell her story based on the three points of difference she noted, highlighting what happened to her that was different. The listeners record six points as before, three similarities and three differences

S/he said, but s/he meant (JH)

An exercise to look at perception in our use of words. The participants select comments that have been made by others and then restate them as they have been understood in their minds. This enables a lack of trust in the facilitators or project organisers to be explored. The facilitators participate also, showing that misunderstandings and miscomprehensions exist on both sides

Significant ages (SU adapted by JH)

Divide into groups of 5 to7. One person in each group stands apart from the others who form a line. She thinks of significant periods in her life, noting the age she was at the time. She then moulds the others into statues representative of herself at each of the ages she has chosen. With this complete, the protagonist passes from one to the other speaking to them, offering advice, warnings, encouragement, whatever is relevant to the age and the event that marked that period of her life. The statues stay frozen and unresponsive throughout. After the protagonist has spoken to the statues individually, they can begin to ask questions, request further clarification or even challenge him but they cannot move. Now they can speak, all the statues are free to talk at the same time so their job is to get the attention of the protagonist. This process is repeated for each individual. Time should be given to the group afterwards, during which they can discuss which version of themselves each was most drawn to and why, which they avoided, which surprised them.

Softly Softly (AB 1995:62-63)

This is used with a prepared scene or a forum presentation. Sometimes a scene can get too violent or out of control and this exercise helps enhance powers of self-observation while allowing the participants' emotions to calm down. The facilitator gives the command 'softly softly' at a moment in the action. The actors must slow down their actions and speak in as low a voice as possible while being audible to those around them. On a command from the facilitator the action resumes at normal speed and volume, as if nothing has happened. The exercise is repeated as many times as is felt necessary at different stages during the scene.

Stop! Think! (AB 2002:227, 1995:61-62)

Used with a prepared scene or a forum presentation. The facilitator stops at a moment in the action. The actors must speak aloud everything in their character's minds without stopping, transforming into words all the thoughts that pass through their heads. This can be done with the facilitator passing from one to another signalling for each to speak their thoughts aloud, or everyone involved in the scene can speak together at the same time, staying focused on themselves and not listening to anyone else in the scene. On a command from the facilitator the action is resumed exactly where it left off, as if nothing has happened. The exercise is repeated as many times as is felt necessary, at different stages during the scene.

Stop! Justify! (a variation on Stop! Think!, adapted by JH)

Used with a prepared scene or a forum presentation. The facilitator stops at a moment in the action and the actors must justify their actions and words as their character. This can be done with the facilitator passing from one to another signalling for each to speak their thoughts aloud, or everyone involved in the scene can speak together at the same time, each staying focused on themselves and not listening to anyone else. On a command from the facilitator the action is resumed exactly where it left off, as if nothing has happened. The exercise is repeated as many times as is felt necessary.

Tag games (SU):

Amoeba – One person is 'it'. The others scatter. If anyone is touched, they join hands or link elbows and continue to chase. The amoeba continues to grow until all are caught. Only the two ends of the amoeba can tag players.

Blob Tag – One person is 'it'. The others scatter. If anyone is touched, they join hands or link elbows and continue to chase. Once the blob reaches 4 people, it splits onto two, and so on until everyone is caught.

Bridge Tag – In pairs the group face each other making a bridge with their arms in the air, hands touching. One person is left out. For that person to be safe, they must duck under the arms of another person and take their place. The person who has been displaced is now being chased.

British Bulldog – One person stands in the middle of the space while the others line up along one wall. The one in the middle calls out 'run' and everyone in the line tries to run safely to other side of the space. If tagged, they help the person in the middle for further rounds, continuing until everyone has been tagged.

Everybody's It – Everyone is 'it' and each person tries to tag before being tagged. If tagged, the person must sit, but if they tag someone else, they are back in the game.

Hug Tag – One person tags the others by touching them on their stomach. If she touches someone they chase the others and the person who tagged them is released. People can only save themselves by hugging one other person (stomach to stomach) for no more than five seconds.

Loose Connection – In groups of 3 or 4, hands are placed on shoulders of person in front and group moves around the space. When the facilitator calls 'loose connection' the groups must let go of their line and find a new one. This continues several times, ensuring players switch roles.

Octopus Tag – Like British Bulldog, but a person who is tagged sits where they got tagged and waves their arms around trying to tag runners going by. If they succeed in tagging someone from the seated position, positions are switched.

Trust based exercises: Noises (SU)
In pairs one partner is blindfolded, the other is her guide. The guide makes a noise and the partner listens and must follow the direction from which the noise is coming. When the guide stops making the noise the blind partner must also stop. The guide should look after the safety of the blind person, stopping them by ceasing the sound if they are in danger, or changing the tone. As confidence grows, guide should move further and further from the blind person.

Trust based exercises: Joe Egg (SU)
The group forms a circle. One person stands in the middle and lets himself fall straight in various directions and is pushed back to the middle by the surrounding group.

Variation: again in groups of 3, but the middle person's feet must stay in the same spot so they can move only backward and forward.

Wheel of Oppression (adaption by JH from AB's Image Theatre work)

Participants are asked to think about oppressors in their lives. The group then forms two concentric circles and each person in the outer circle sculpts an image, using her partner's body, to represent her oppressor. Participants are asked to focus on triggers that cause people to react to a person before they have even spoken. Triggers can be the way someone stands, the way they look or hold their head and hands, how they place their arms, even a raised eyebrow. Once sculpted, the oppressor must remain frozen while the sculptors walk around to observe other images, discussing similarities and differences. The sculptors then address their sculpted oppressors, over a five-minute period, telling them things they have always wanted to, asking questions, even challenging them. The statues then come alive and, drawing on the knowledge gained by how they were moulded and what is said to them, they respond as the oppressor they believe themselves to be. A conversation begins. The inner circle becomes the outer circle and the process is repeated. Discussions afterwards take place between partners and then in a general feedback with the group as a whole.

Wind Up (SU adapted by JH)

A topic for discussion is chosen and the group pretend they are clockwork people and have a particular opinion or agenda. As they are wound up they must exhaust everything they feel this person would say on the issue, talking as they believe that person or type of person would. When they have exhausted the topic they wind down and come to a stop. They can only speak on the topic again if they are wound up. This exercise often leads to the stereotyping of identities and this is a good point for discussion.

Variation: instead of individuals taking turns, a number of people can be wound up at the same time to see how the interactions will play out.

Theatre versus Oppression

Theatre versus Oppression (TVO) began operations in late 2000 as an informal grouping of like-minded people who wanted to use forms of theatre in issue-based situations in their free time. In 2007 TVO gained charitable status in the UK (registration number SC039092) and has increased its work from this period. Projects are taken on annually depending on grants awarded and funds raised. TVO also runs training courses throughout the year to help support its charitable activities. All those working for TVO do so on a voluntary basis and undergo training and ongoing development both within and outside of the projects. For full information on TVO activities and plays please see www.theatreversusoppression.com.

A summary of TVO plays
All plays can be purchased from Theatre versus Oppressio
www.theatreversus oppression.com

'Til Death do us Part (2011) *(available in Spanish and English)*
A one act play developed using Theatre of the Oppressed techniques after a series of workshops with victims and perpetrators of domestic abuse in the UK and USA. The goal of the play is to explore conflict in relationships, not only marital relationships. Designed for a cast of two in which the actors speak directly to the audience. The play at no point takes sides and creates a level of discomfort as we come to acknowledge that the situation is not as black and white as we would like to believe it to be.

The Sin Eater (2006) *(available in Spanish and English)*
The play is written for two characters – the torturer, who represents many different torturers, and the interviewer. The scenery consists of two chairs and a table with a simple cloth, a jug of water and two glasses. The play centres on memories and material from interviews – some semi-fabricated to protect certain individuals, most factual – with guards and torturers from dictatorships in South America. The factual

accounts have not been attributed and the torturer remains nameless deliberately to emphasise how he can be anyone anywhere; that his monstrous acts do not give him a monstrous appearance. He could easily be the person standing next to us waiting for the bus or sitting next to us in a café, a neighbour, someone we work beside, even a member of our own family.

The Art of Silence (2005) *(available in Spanish and English)*

The play, a psychological political drama, is based on actor Emilio Barreto's experiences in prison over a thirteen year period. He was held without charge through these years by the dictatorial regime of his country, eight years of which he spent in a single cell of 2.5 metres by 4, in which up to 12 others were imprisoned at any given time. The play follows the different stages of resistance and acceptance, of struggle and relinquishment that Emilio experienced during the eight year period of cell confinement and how he tried to keep his mind active and his imagination free. It aims to show, indirectly, the effect of the imprisonment and torture on an individual, the means used to survive, the nature of that survival and its mental and physical cost. Two characters are involved, a young Emilio experiencing the horror of his situation and an older Emilio remembering and, at times, attempting to communicate with his younger self through movement and mime.

Real Voices (2004) *(available in English only)*

Real Voices was a play commissioned by UNIFEM to explore oppression in women worldwide. Using a mixture of transcript and news footage, the stories of women from all corners of the world are brought together unified by the oppression they face whether it be rape and domestic violence in the UK or female genital mutilation and arranged marriages in Africa. The extracts are placed together like the pieces of a jigsaw emphasising the strength and bravery of women the world over. This play was written as an educational piece with the intention to instruct.

Cabezas Dislocadas (1998) *(available in Spanish only)*

Cabezas Dislocadas (Dislocated Heads) was first performed in Asunción, Paraguay in 1998. The play is a highly polemical look at the stereotype attitudes that are firmly grounded in many South American societies. The story tells of a troubled family and the attitudes that dominated the post-dictatorship era: the fear of the past dictatorship and the current democracy; the politics never spoken of and the torture and imprisonment that accompanied it; the concept of a favoured child; a loveless marriage; class distinction; the prohibition of homosexuality and the unfulfilled dreams. Encapsulated in one family we watch how these different aspects come into play, the destructive nature of unspoken thoughts and words that finally reach crisis point.